unseen

muwanga

Trilogy Christian Publishers
A Wholly Owned Subsidary of Trinity Broadcasting Network
2442 Michelle Drive, Tustin, CA 92780

10 9 8 7 6 5 4 3 2 1
Library of Congress Cataloging-in-Publication Data is available.
ISBN 978-1-64088-451-9 (Print Book)
ISBN 978-1-64088-452-6 (ebook)

contents

foreword

To say that the early days of planting a church were difficult would be an understatement. For example, there was the time early in our ministry where we had recently moved into our first building. Given that I had begun my ministry by standing under a tree preaching to passerby, moving into a physical building was a significant and exciting milestone. The Lord had called me to plant a church in the heart of a Muslim village in Africa, and while I didn't necessarily expect to be received with open arms, I also didn't expect to be greeted with a hand grenade. It was an act of hate and evil that left several dead and many others wounded. I was one of the wounded and nearly lost my life that day. I will discuss this event and its significance in greater detail later in the book, but I begin with this to set the stage for something I would like for you to think about as you read this book and that is the importance that one's worldview has on his or her life.

In short, a worldview is a collection of beliefs that defines one's existence in the world. Our views about humanity, ethics, religion, and the meaning of life shape how we interact with the world around us and the choices we make on a daily basis. Within our worldview, we form a mental structure that helps organize our basic beliefs into a comprehensive view of what we consider real, good, valuable, helpful, and so on. Whoever threw that grenade clearly had a worldview that included and supported the belief that killing innocent people was justified.

Experiences largely shape our worldviews, and there are many different points of view that exist in our world today due to people's different experiences in the world. While we often cannot control these experiences, we can control how we process and respond to them. People in Africa often have very different life experiences than people in western countries; therefore, they often see the world and the spiritual realm very differently than their western counterparts. As I know that many reading this book may never make it to Africa, I feel that reading this material is the next best thing one can do to understand how the African lifestyle informs the African spiritual perspective. It is my hope that you will take a personal inventory of how you view the world as you read this book and that the decisions you make and your ability to love people will both move in a positive direction.

Because these worldviews shape our opinions and beliefs about how we should interact with the world around us, it is rare for us to act outside of the boundaries of our worldview. Depending on one's worldview, this can either be a good thing or a detrimental one. For example, my life experiences in both the kingdom of darkness and the kingdom of light have led me to the conclusion that seeing the world from a Christian perspective is the most beneficial both for the individual and for the surrounding world. I understand that most have not and will not have the life experiences to shape the same worldview that I have; however, I do believe that the material in this book has the power to significantly broaden and change your worldview if you are willing to lend it proper consideration.

There is a spiritual war going on for the soul of every human being on earth. The Bible talks clearly about this war, stating in Ephesians 6:12 that "we do not wrestle against flesh and blood, but against principalities, against powers, against the rulers of the darkness of this age, against spiritual hosts of wickedness in the heavenly places." This reality often goes overlooked, particularly in parts of the world where material prosperity is commonplace. This is dangerous both during one's life on earth and in his or her existence eternally. Failure to recognize these realities leaves an individual open to and unprotected from attacks from Satan and his demonic realm. In the pages that follow, I will expose you to the reality of spiritual warfare and discuss some of the effects that it has on both the lives of individuals and the world as a whole.

In any event where two or more entities are involved in a struggle against each other, preparation is a vital component for the victor. Successful sports teams often spend hours watching film and discussing what they think will be the strategy of their next opponent. Successful lawyers spend hours poring over details about the opposition in hopes they won't be caught off-guard by an unforeseen accusation or piece of information. Even when the adversary is inanimate, such as a test for school, one would be unwise and naïve to assume success if he or she doesn't study the material for the exam. The point is that if success is often a by-product of preparation, then the same principal applies to the spiritual war waged against us. For some reason, though, perhaps because it deals with what is unseen, many overlook and fail to familiarize themselves with the tactics of the enemy. In turn, their resulting worldview reflects this lack of spiritual knowledge.

I will discuss this in greater detail later in the book, but, in short, Satan seeks to destroy as much as he can on earth in the time he has until God's ultimate victory and cleansing of all that is evil. Because people are God's chosen instrument for the advancement of His kingdom on earth, Satan and his demons direct their attacks against the people God created. Satan is a deceiver. He doesn't want you or me to know he exists. Why? Because if we do know and are familiar with his motives, strategies, and tactics then we are far more likely to be successful in not only personal victory against his attacks but also more effective in the work we do for the Kingdom of God and its advancement.

If our worldview largely dictates the decisions we make and how we interact with the world, then surely this spiritual knowledge is important. It has the power to change our decisions and interactions with God's created world. More specifically, the impact of this knowledge is particularly significant because religion plays such an essential role in shaping and defining one's worldview.

If you are either not religious or are the adherent of a religion other than Christianity, I am so glad that you are reading this book. I pray that what follows both encourages you and challenges you to consider the life-changing and life-giving transformation that a relationship with Jesus Christ brings. For the believer in Christ reading this book, I am also so glad that you are here. It is also my hope and prayer that what follows will encourage and challenge you. Furthermore, I pray that it moves you to a deeper love for and greater fellowship with our Lord and Savior Jesus Christ.

In Christ,
Muwanga

SECTION ONE

muwanga's life

chapter one:
muwanga

MY EARLY LIFE

My name is Muwanga. My story begins in a small African village in the late 1950s. One of six children born to unwed parents, I grew up in a family marked by serious dysfunction. My father was an alcoholic who cared much more about his drinking than providing for the needs of a wife and kids. This drinking frequently led to violence, which was often directed toward my mother. The violence became bad enough that one day she left and took my youngest sibling with her. As she saw it, she had to take action to survive. She left the rest of us with my father. Not surprisingly, once she left our situation worsened. The drinking continued, and the neglect increased. Food became scarce and malnutrition commonplace, and starvation slowly crept into our reality. When my mother heard about our situation, she came back to the village to save us from my father. In a sense, this was accomplished. Had we stayed in the village with my father we likely would have died of starvation, abuse, or a combination of both; moving away, however, did not remove the struggle.

I was five years old at the time all of this happened. Needless to say, this was difficult to process, but like many children, I just assumed that my situation was normal. Upon moving to the new village, all of us worked at odd jobs but still found it difficult to put food on the table. It is also important to note that during this time I was coming of age to go to school. My siblings were already old enough, and as is to be expected, this put an additional burden on my mother. Ultimately, we could not afford to pay for school, and I was left with very little formal education.

Once I was old enough to somewhat grasp my plight, I decided to return to my father's village. When I arrived, I found out that my father was dead. In addition to his alcoholism, he had also been deeply involved in witchcraft.

The combination of my father's death and my return to his village prompted the start of my involvement in witchcraft. I was introduced to my grandfather shortly after learning of my father's death. He lived in a nearby village where he was a witchdoctor and warmly welcomed me upon my arrival. He was a very well-respected member of the community and had a reputation for being a kind man who welcomed needy people who came to him for help. On the other hand, they also knew he was a tremendously powerful witchdoctor with deadly Satanic abilities.

I realize many readers are not at all familiar with African culture, tribal practices, or witchdoctors. Thus, I feel it is important to note that there will be times in this story when I will break from the narrative to explain something essential to understanding the story in depth. This is one of those instances.

ROLE OF A WITCHDOCTOR

I have just mentioned that my father was heavily involved in witchcraft and that my grandfather was a practicing witchdoctor. He was an agent of the devil and was possessed by demons who used him to do supernatural things. Because of a witchdoctor's access to the supernatural realm, people in a village may go to the witchdoctor for a wide variety of reasons. Some may go for physical healing of a disease or sickness (done through the use of herbs) or healing of a strained relationship. Others may go in hopes of obtaining material prosperity. One way that material prosperity is gained is through promotion at work. The hope is that the witchdoctor will manipulate their work situation in a way to accomplish this for them. In other instances, people will seek the services of the witchdoctor in order to have an enemy killed.

Witchdoctors can cause or cure many problems ranging from, but not limited to, disease, poverty, division, hatred, strife, and conflict. The successful performance of various ceremonies, rituals, and sacrifices is often required before carrying out a specific evil task. They can also get involved in situations where killings are requested. Satan usually gives or approves the details involved in killing people. We often see these events as unexplained accidents, suicide, strange illnesses, and murders, among other things. In order to carry out these assignments, the witchdoctors enter into the supernatural realm and meet with the demons assigned to them. These demons often take the shape of what the witchdoctors and villagers refer to as their "ancestral spirits." Because the demons live in the spiritual dimension, they are able to see the personal problems of both the person requesting help and also the enemies being targeted. My grandfather spent significant amounts of time with demons nearly every day. He received instructions from Satan through these demons. The demons then assisted in carrying out the various evil tasks villagers had requested in their local area.

Demons are territorial. Usually, the most powerful demons in a village area will pick what is known as a "high place," such as a mountaintop, as their headquarters. The villagers eventually learn to stay away from such places because they are very dangerous.

WITCHDOCTOR'S INFLUENCE

Each village is likely to have several witchdoctors living and practicing there. Usually, each one has a different level of effectiveness. The most reliable and powerful ones are the most popular. The influence that a witchdoctor has in a community is often deep-seated and intricate. I will divide the areas of influence into the following three categories: historical, physical, and spiritual.

The first area of influence I will discuss is the historical. When I speak of the influence one has over a village, it is important to remember and consider that these villages are often in rural, isolated areas. This plays a significant role in the influence of the witchdoctor. For example, if there is no strong Christian church or strong spiritual Christians in a village, then the local witchdoctor has likely been the dominant spiritual authority in that area for a long time. In the typical unchurched village, witchdoctors may have been the only significant spiritual influence for hundreds of years. In contrast, in America many may find themselves in areas that may have a dominant spiritual influence but not an area solely occupied by one specific religious teaching or belief system. For example, those living in the American South, commonly known as the "Bible Belt," might say that their community tends to have a dominant evangelical Christian influence. However, in any of these communities one would likely find multiple denominations with slightly different teachings. These varied teachings often lead to different manifestations of lifestyle. To clarify, for instance, Pentecostals, Presbyterians, Baptists, and Methodists believe that in order to have fellowship and eternal life with God, one must believe that Jesus Christ was crucified and rose from the dead to save from sin those who believe in Him. However, differences in, say, beliefs about the manifestation of spiritual gifts lead to Sunday morning services in these respective churches looking quite different from one another.

In addition to different denominations of Christian churches, many of these communities may have established groups of other practicing religions. I say all this to make the point that in Western society, people are frequently exposed to others with different life experiences and religious beliefs, thus allowing the individual the ability to choose what he or she believes to be true and of highest importance. In remote, historically impoverished villages in Africa, this melting pot of culture and religious influence is highly uncommon. This leaves the witch-doctor with a platform for monopolizing spiritual belief systems.

Alongside the historical reality of influence, there is also the physical reality of what is seen and experienced living under the authority of an evil leader. The villagers have long been recipients or observers of numerous evil acts and are well aware of the evil power flowing through the witchdoctor. In other words, they have seen physically-tangible manifestations of works of evil leading them to believe in and submit to the authority and power of the one through whom these acts flow and manifest.

Another area of physical influence deals with that gained by socioeconomic status. A witchdoctor is often among the wealthiest members of his community. As with nearly all other forms of service, there is payment involved anytime a witchdoctor renders service as a result of a villager's request. In view of the types of services performed, these payments generally come in the form of money, some form of livestock, or other items of value. The fact that this standing in society draws villagers' attention and respect should come as no surprise. It is human nature to ascribe extra value to people based upon socioeconomic status and material wealth. Many associate material wealth with power, intelligence, happiness, and importance. We think those that have such things must be happy and content. Think of how the world treats celebrities, whether they be musicians, actors, athletes, politicians, or highly successful business people. We often believe, almost without question, what they say and do and model ourselves after their words and behaviors. For example, imagine an athletic company approaching a highly successful athlete in hopes that he or she will become an endorser of their product. Why does the company do this? Because they know that if that celebrity-status athlete endorses their product, sales will go up. Why? Because people want to be like that athlete. We want to run faster, jump higher, and look as they do because the ability to do these things has brought them importance, wealth, and higher value.

I give this example to point to the nature of human beings. This inclination to ascribe extra importance to someone with material wealth is found in America, impoverished African villages, and everywhere in between. Since witchdoctors often have greater material wealth than the rest of those in the community, it is natural for people to be inclined to believe and value what they say and do.

FEAR'S INFLUENCE

The historical, physical, and spiritual combination of influence all unite under the umbrella of fear. Ultimately, fear is what keeps the stronghold of darkness and oppression over those who live in submission to the witchdoctor's manifestations. It may be tempting to pass this off as cheap superstition, but take a moment to consider the role that fear plays in the human condition. Whether consciously or subconsciously, humans are drawn to fear. Most would probably admit that, to some extent, they have a fear of the unknown, and this is one of the major premises by which fear operates and successfully preys upon its victims. Consider this comparison of witchcraft to the news media. The news media lives and dies by successful ratings, and these ratings, some would argue, often revolve around a fear of the unknown. This is one reason the overwhelming majority of the news is so negative. It often appears that these stations hook people and draw them into a cyclical pattern of viewing due to the individual's desire to know more about the unknown and thereby achieve more control over his or her own domain. Let me explain.

THE DESIRE TO SELF-PRESERVE

Let's say that a convenience store is robbed in the city where you live, but it happens in a part of the city that you rarely visit. Knowing that the overwhelming majority of people in the city were not and typically will not be affected by this, the media is still quick to report the crime and often will feature the story on their television segment or their website. Why? First, because a robbery is a frightening experience, and they know that, generally speaking, more people would rather know about this than, say, a local school having a successful fundraiser. Why? Because knowledge of a robbery evokes both uncertainty and a desire for control and gives people an outlet for, in their mind, gaining control of their domain. What I mean by this is that when people become aware of the robbery, a situation that is out of their control, they realize that they could potentially become a victim of a similar crime, and this causes fear, even if somewhat subconscious and unnoticed. They then realize that the best they can do to control the situation is to avoid that part of town and that convenience store and, experiencing some degree of relief, return to a state of normalcy. But what if another robbery happens, and they don't find out about it, and because of their lack of knowledge, go to that part of town or that store and get robbed themselves? So they continuously pay attention to the media in order to do all they can to promote this cycle of information gathering for protection and self-preservation, thereby gaining more control of their domain.

In effect, the reasons for going to a witchdoctor are much the same. People go in an attempt to acquire more knowledge and gain some higher level of control. At its core, it is just another form of self-preservation. Consider the aforementioned reasons that people request the services of a witchdoctor: various types of healing, financial increase, and vengeance. In the instance of healing, for example, the intent behind going to the witchdoctor is to gain knowledge of what is wrong, the cause of the problem, and the solution to the problem. This is both addressing the fear of the unknown and attempting to gain control of one's personal domain. In the mind of the client, he or she is acknowledging that something is out of his or her control and making a conscious decision to rectify it. Often, the witchdoctor will then draw the client into a cyclical pattern of returning and rendering payments for the improvement to be ongoing. He will inform the client of what rituals need to be performed or what spells or curses need to be cast for protection to continue. For these acts to be performed, the witchdoctor will require payment for materials and services, and the client, desperate and often with a deep belief in the witchdoctor's ability to dictate circumstance, returns over and over again to satisfy fear and gain control over his or her situation. Much like the example of the news station reporting a robbery, the witchdoctor provides the same type of emotional effect upon a person, but on a much deeper, more consciously-aware level.

———————

MY FIRST SPIRITUAL ENCOUNTER

I walked to my grandfather's house the same day I learned of my father's death. He only lived about five miles from my father's village and was very happy to see me when I arrived. Whether or not he had been expecting me I'm not sure, but he wasted no time in introducing me to witchcraft. The morning after my first night with him, he asked me to accompany him to meet his ancestral spirit in a hut near his house. This hut served as a shrine. Put simply, a shrine is a structure that both houses the materials used to perform rituals and sacrifices and the place where these rituals and sacrifices occur. When we entered the shrine, he taught me the song we would be singing and how to help him and participate in the ceremonies. Then, he began playing a drum, and we started singing. As we were singing, a snake came out from behind a large cloth curtain and began moving in my general direction. The best way I know to describe it is that the snake had a medium-sized body with a very oddly shaped head. Being a young boy at the time, this nearly caused me to abandon the meeting. Had it not been for my grandfather's comforting words before the meeting I most likely would have. He told me before we went in that our ancestral spirits would come to receive me in the form of a snake and two millipedes. There was no reason for me to be afraid.

When the snake appeared, my grandfather blinked his eyes at me as if to remind me of our conversation. My nerves settled a bit, and I sat back and tried to convince myself that my grandfather would not lead me into anything that would harm me. Then I heard a deep voice come from the place where the snake was located. The voice said, "My grandson and my servant, thank you for coming. I have chosen you to be my servant, and you are going to serve me with your grandfather. You will help my people with their problems with sickness, poverty, and personal enemies. I will protect you, and I will kill your enemies. I will make you rich and give you many wives and children." After these words my grandfather instructed me to sing the same song we sang earlier. The voice then said to my grandfather, "Whenever you come to the meeting, you shouldn't leave Muwanga behind." After this, the meeting was over, and I left very encouraged. I came out different than when I entered. I walked in poor, discouraged, and hopeless. I was a young boy with a mother who struggled to provide, a father who was dead, and the equivalent of a third-grade education. I had just been told that I would be protected, made rich, and given a family. Submission to this authority was an easy sell.

MY GRANDFATHER'S INFLUENCE

After my encounter with the ancestral spirit, my grandfather spent a great deal of time with me every day telling me stories, which were very unsettling and scary at times, about these ancestral spirits. He told me that they killed people and that they would torture him whenever he rebelled against them. It soon became very clear that my grandfather was controlled by someone or something far beyond his control. I was about fifteen years old at this time, and during this period of my life, I was always with him. I did everything from go with him during his ministry to the sick and needy to accompany him during the offering of animal sacrifices. As might be expected, this was a very formative time in my life. This was the first time that I had been taught by a mature and caring person. My grandfather's consistency and mentorship was something I needed and desired.

CONTACT IN HIGH PLACES

Our country is divided into five regions: northern, southern, eastern, western, and central. In each of these regions, the residing tribe has a "high place," usually on a mountaintop, that they consider to be a source of strength and the foundation of their tribal worship. Our tribe is from the central region, so that is where the most revered mountain of our tribe is located. It is believed that our ancestral spirits established our tribe from the tops of these mountains and still reside there. Most tribal people are afraid to go up on these mountains unless they are with people who are devoted to serving these demons. This fear is legitimate due to the fact that if an unauthorized tribal member wanders onto these demonic "high places" they may very well be killed.

DISTANT SPIRITUAL MEETINGS

My grandfather informed me that we would be going to meet with higher-level ancestral spirits to start my training to become a witchdoctor. To be clear, I already had plenty of exposure to the world of witchcraft through my time with my grandfather, but it's not exactly a process where one merely signs up and then just naturally "becomes." Like most things, it takes time, training, and instruction to hone one's skill. I had a lot to learn.

My grandfather told me that we would be going to our tribe's high place in preparation for the meeting. The following day we would be going to meet with the ancestral spirits, and my training would begin. So the next day, we traveled up the mountain and spent an entire day and night there. During this period, we fasted the entire time. I had consumed no food or drink during the entire trip. This was because the ancestral spirits don't eat natural food. Instead, they tend to be fond of human flesh and blood. We didn't have to consume human matter to meet with them, but, to be sensitive to them and enter the meeting with the appropriate frame of mind, we had to fast.

Upon returning from the trip to the high place, my grandfather and I prepared to make the long journey to the spirit world. In his house was a "strong room," which nobody was allowed to enter except my grandfather and me. This room was where the ritual was performed for the transport to the place where we would meet with higher-ranking ancestral spirits and many demons themselves. Once in the strong room, my grandfather pulled down a python snake skin and spread it on the floor. He asked me to sit on the tail while he sat on the head. He made incantations, or prayers, and then we disappeared from the hut and travelled spiritually to the shores of the Indian Ocean on the other side of India.

If asked for a detailed explanation of how we got there, I could not give one. There are some things that I have experienced that I simply cannot explain, and this is one of those experiences. I am not sure whether we traveled with or without our physical bodies, but my grandfather had done this many times, and I simply relied on what he told me. Although spiritual travel is not something many Westerners know much about, it is rather common among various third-world religions.

We soon arrived at the meeting place, which was beneath the Indian Ocean. Both humans and demons were present. None of us needed air to breathe. During the meeting, no human was allowed to speak, ask questions, laugh, etc. We weren't allowed to do anything. A massive demonic figure addressed us. Whether or not it was Satan I'm not sure, but he gave us the evil authority and power we would need to do our evil work. He also instructed each of us in the meeting as to what we would be doing and how to do it. If he had been a human, he would have stood about twenty feet tall and weighed around five-hundred pounds; he was terrifying. A good deal of the instruction dealt with killing people. We were instructed on how to kill by bewitching, striking people with lightning, and causing accidents and other tragic scenarios leading to death. We were also taught how to deal with those who came to us for help and how to provide services to them. Lastly, we were taught how to confuse and cause division within communities. After the demonic figure spoke to us at this undersea meeting, I realized it was the same voice I heard from the snake in my grandfather's shrine.

chapter two:
life as a witchdoctor

My return from the first meeting under the sea signaled the start of my career as a witchdoctor. It is probably easy to assume that when someone becomes a witchdoctor there is a big ceremony or right-of-passage celebration. This, however, is not necessarily the case. When I returned from the first meeting, the most important matter at hand was completing my first task, not celebrating. I don't remember the first thing I did, but I do know that the completion of these tasks is how the members of a community become informed of a new witchdoctor in an area. Word tends to travel quickly when someone is effective at their craft, and I was effective because of my grandfather's detailed guidance. I was about sixteen at this time and still had a lot to learn, but I was headed toward a successful career.

As I attempt to explain how this all works, there are two words that I think will be helpful for you to think about as you process what follows: partnership and cyclical. Think of partnership as a working relationship between two entities, whether they be spiritual or physical, and think of cyclical in terms of similar things happening repeatedly.

There are two important partnerships that exist for the witchdoctor to be successful in his craft. One is the partnership between the witchdoctor and the demons assigned to him, and the other is the partnership with the client, or patient. I use the word "partnership" here to point to the fact that in both instances there is a working, almost professional nature to the relationship. I think this is best seen in an example of a typical interaction between a patient and a witchdoctor.

PARTNERS AT WORK

In a typical scenario, a patient would come to me with a problem. When they came to me, I would invite them in, and they would try to explain their problem. At this point, I would bring out a basket of shells that had been formerly used as Arabian currency. The shells themselves held no particular significance; they were merely a physical representation of the unseen spiritual forces at work. The patients, however, believed that the shells revealed something important. I would shake the shells around in my hand and then roll them like dice, which summoned the presence of the evil spirit to come upon me. The demon would then speak through me to diagnose the problem of the patient. Once I identified the problem, I would inform the patient of how much my services would cost.

SACRIFICES

Anytime someone calls upon the services of a witchdoctor, a sacrifice is involved. If the sacrifice is not currency, then it is its equivalent. For lower-level requests, the equivalent often comes in the form of livestock. For higher-level requests, often in addition to something of monetary value, blood is involved.

Getting a job, healing of an illness, having a child, requesting abnormal sexual favors, bewitching a neighbor or family member, and asking for protection fall into the category of lower-level requests. This is because the stakes aren't as high for these types of jobs. Generally speaking, for a witchdoctor and the demons to effectively carry out a task of this nature, human death isn't necessary. Since nobody else has to die for these tasks to be carried out successfully, human death isn't required to complete them. In many of these cases, a client would be asked to sacrifice a chicken, goat, or cow. For sexual requests, a client would normally be asked to provide six to ten goats.

Although in the same category, asking for protection carries greater weight than other lower-level requests. For a protection job, a client would be required to provide no less than five cows. For someone in extreme poverty, this is quite a large sacrifice. When payment is received, the witchdoctor will then assign the client a demon to protect him or her from harm. The killing of another person is not the intention of this type of request, but if it is necessary for protection then the demons will kill.

Monetary gain, political power, and/or the killing of another person fall into the category of high-level requests. One reason for this is because, if carried out successfully, they separate the client from normal society. If someone becomes rich or attains political power, he or she ascends the social ladder, thereby leaving the poverty from which he or she often comes. The killing of another person also separates a client because it is the highest-level request one can make.

To carry out these high-level requests, witchdoctors require human blood. This is because the shedding of blood is the highest form of sacrifice. It shows the utmost obedience and devotion of both the client and witchdoctor to Satan. This is because human-beings are God's highest form of creation, so to kill a human is to kill God's most precious creation. We will get into this later in the "References" section, but this is one of the reasons why Jesus Christ's death on the cross was the ultimate sacrifice. God humbled Himself, took on the form of His most precious creation, and shed human blood to atone for the sins of His people.

If a villager wanted to become rich, he or she may be required to kill his or her family members and bring the blood to the witchdoctor, who would then instruct the client to drink it. Similarly, clients who wanted to attain political power would normally be required to kill someone, bring the blood to the witchdoctor, and drink it.

The highest-level request, the killing of another person, required the largest payment: the sacrifice of a newborn baby. As I write this now, it is difficult to acknowledge that this actually happens. It is true evidence of not only Satan's desire to harm people at all costs but also of the hardening of one's heart that can occur when he or she surrenders completely to the desires of the flesh. To require the death of a newborn baby from parents who have been anticipating the child's birth and love him or her deeply demonstrates the ultimate disregard for human life. This is perhaps the most telling example of the depth to which people in many third-world countries are enslaved to witchcraft. The parents undoubtedly love their newborn child, but their way of thinking has been so warped by Satan that they are willing to sacrifice their own child for personal gain. This is what Satan wants and, unfortunately, what he gets when man chooses to live in complete opposition to life and salvation in Jesus Christ.

So, in these examples, you can see the partnership aspect at work. In the witchdoctor/patient partnership, the patient relies on the witchdoctor for his abilities and services, and the witchdoctor relies on the patient's problem for income. In the case of the witchdoctor/demon partnership, the witchdoctor calls upon the demons to facilitate the completion of the services requested, and the demons rely on the witchdoctor for instructions on how to do so.

THE CYCLE

In addition to the partnership element of these engagements, many times there is a cyclical nature as well. I touched on this in the first chapter, but I will expound on it here. If you recall, in the last chapter I discussed the nature in which many view the news media. Many people constantly return to the media out of an attempt to gain control of their domain. In many ways, the witchdoctor serves as a similar figure in the life of his clients. The clients go to the witchdoctor with their problem, and then they are drawn into a cycle of returning in order for the healing, protection, promotion, etc. to continue. Even in the example of having someone killed for protection, the seed is planted for that client to return if another problem arises. Additionally, the clients have seen the completion of the task and have no reason to believe that the same couldn't happen to them. They often then get trapped in a cycle of fear.

As you might imagine, this keeps the individual from Christ. This is why the cyclical nature is so important to the mission of Satan and his demons. Isolated events can be powerful, but repeated events are the ones that often define people's lives. For example, forgetting to study for one test usually doesn't determine whether someone passes or fails a class. However, if someone chooses to repeatedly neglect his or her studies, then failure is almost certain. In the case of a witchdoctor's clients, if they repeatedly return to witchcraft then that means they aren't turning to Christ, which is a victory for the kingdom of darkness.

Witchdoctors also often use their demons to create problems, which undoubtedly keeps them in business. An example of the cyclical nature of the witchdoctor's practice, one that is extremely prevalent in many African communities, is the transmission of HIV. This often happens when an attractive woman comes to the witchdoctor as a patient. It is not uncommon for the woman to have sexual relations with the witchdoctor as either part of the payment or as an independent act. Either way, this is one reason why witchdoctors are so effective at spreading HIV. Once successful transmission of the disease occurs and symptoms arise, you can probably guess what happens next. The woman comes back to the witchdoctor for healing, and thus, the cycle continues.

DAILY LIFE

Now, I may have created an image in your mind that witchdoctors and their demons go around wreaking havoc in broad daylight. While there is some truth to this, it's not necessarily that obvious to the public eye. It's not as if they just walk around and point at buildings and make them collapse or pick up cars and throw them across the street. In other words, I don't want you to have this image of a cinematic villain walking around openly terrorizing the community because that would not be accurate. Remember that witchdoctors are often highly respected and valued members of their communities, and many of the tasks they complete are a result of interactions with personal clients.

This may leave you wondering what life looks like for a witchdoctor. Albeit different than an "ordinary" existence, the day-to-day life of a witchdoctor is more normal than one might imagine.

Like other people, witchdoctors eat food, drink water, and work to support their families. I will discuss this at greater detail in the next chapter, but there was a point for me where my practice as a witchdoctor was suffering so bad that I had to go look for other work. In other words, witchdoctors are not automatically guaranteed a prosperous life just because they have supernatural abilities. In addition, there are often other local witchdoctors with similar abilities that may be more effective than others in certain areas. This creates competition, which means that if you don't perform well business suffers.

Also, some may assume that witchdoctors live alone, which makes sense. Who would want to live with someone whose life is defined by deep immersion in the Satanic realm? While this is a valid thought, many witchdoctors have wives and children. Everything looks normal, and the family is fully aware of the demonic powers at work. However, the evil activities are usually done in the witchdoctor's shrine, which is usually off-limits to other members of the family. This often preserves a sense of normalcy within the house. One thing that is not as normal, however, is that at any time the witchdoctor can decide to bring another woman into the family as a wife. This is generally accepted with little pushback due to the fear of the husband's power.

Witchdoctors also generally have the same wants and needs as other people, and they use their demonic power for personal gain. For example, let's say that I had a specific interest in a piece of land. If I wanted the land bad enough, I might cause an illness to fall on the landowner to the point where he had to come to me for help. When he came to me, I might require his payment to be that piece of land. If he refused, the illness would get worse. Eventually, I would acquire the land, which would further solidify my position as a person of authority in the community.

————————

For the first five years or so of my practice as a witchdoctor, things went pretty well. I was young, but I was under the constant eye of my grandfather. During this time, he taught me much of what he knew and kept a close watch to make sure that I completed tasks appropriately. His counsel was a major reason for my success. Whenever I had a problem or was confused about how to navigate a certain situation, he was always there to guide me. Little did I know that this relationship that had been such a defining factor in my life would soon come to an end.

chapter three:
called by conversion

During my time as a witchdoctor, I lived and worked in a very isolated area. In fact, the location was so remote that I was never exposed to Christianity or the name of Jesus. I was only familiar with demons, their nature, and their hierarchy. This may come as a surprise, but during my time working for the kingdom of darkness Jesus was never referred to by His name, only as "that man." Even if His name was uttered during a meeting, the chaos that followed was so great that it disrupted our understanding of the significance of His name. The only hope for me or the people in my village would have been the voice of an outsider coming in and proclaiming the message of the gospel. Although I didn't know it at the time, I had already been exposed to the person who would eventually share this message with me, but more on that in a minute.

The isolation of my village lent itself not only to a lack of outside ideas but also to a complete and total reinforcement of the ideas and teachings that were taught to me. As I have said, during this time my grandfather was the source of these teachings. The effect of this was that my world was only as big as my exposure, and my exposure was limited to my village and my grandfather's knowledge.

When I was twenty-one, my grandfather was killed by rampaging soldiers. My survival left me as the go-to witchdoctor in the village, and I was quickly confronted with the reality that I may not have been as cut out for the job as I thought. Although my grandfather taught me a great deal about being a witchdoctor, he didn't reveal all his secrets. It did not take long for me or the villagers to realize that I couldn't do some of the things he did. This gradually destroyed the confidence of the villagers I had been serving, and a significant lack of work soon followed. With the decline in work came a decline in money. It became so bad that I had to leave the village and look for employment elsewhere. I was willing to do any type of work at this point; I was that desperate.

Also during this time, I contracted a mysterious illness that I could not shake. In short, the best way I know to describe it is that there was a burning sensation in my small toe, and my skin looked like snake skin and took over both sides of my body. It brought me a great deal of discomfort and affected me to the point where other people in the village took notice. For the first time in my life, I could not overcome a problem with the demonic beings and techniques that I had access to as a witchdoctor. This further reinforced the villagers' lack of confidence in me and added fuel to the fire of my growing unemployment.

ENCOUNTERING AN OLD FRIEND

The search for work eventually led me to a childhood friend that I had known before becoming involved in witchcraft. My circumstance of illness and unemployment naturally had a way of lessening my pride, so when I encountered this friend I had no problem informing him of my situation. I didn't go too far into specifics, but I did let him know that my personal problems had left me in quite a desperate state.

He listened intently and told me that he thought he could help me. When he offered his solution, I was a bit confused, primarily because I didn't know what he was talking about. He told me to come to church. At least, that was the starting point for the solution. I had no idea what a church was or what it did. My friend explained it to me as best as he could, and I decided that I had nothing to lose. Even though I wasn't sure how going to a place where people sang songs and listened to somebody talk about a man named Jesus would help, I had nowhere else to turn. I agreed to go to church, and with this agreement my friend committed to helping me pursue employment and healing.

As soon as the pact was made, he began to share with me about the same man that he said the preacher talked about. I wasn't sure what this had to do with anything, but he was very intent on making sure that I understood the message. Upon his completion of the gospel presentation, he asked if I was ready to accept Jesus as my Lord and Savior. I must have had a look of bewilderment on my face because he began a second attempt to explain things more clearly. Perhaps it was my preoccupied concern for employment, but today was not the day of salvation. I also explained to him that this Holy Spirit he kept referring to was not in my family, but that didn't seem to do much to deter him. Either way, I just wanted to get to the church.

After these couple of unsuccessful attempts at converting me, we decided to go to the church to meet with the pastor. The pastor repeated this gospel message, but it was getting late, and I still wasn't having it. I wasn't necessarily rude but more disinterested due to my current preoccupations. Also, it had been a long day, and it was getting late. I needed to get home. Realizing this, the pastor gave me some food and some money to pay for the bus fare.

Had the pastor not extended this very generous act of kindness, I may not have returned to the church. Generally speaking, African pastors have very little material and monetary resources, so the food and the bus fare displayed genuine care and concern. I could tell that there was clearly something different about this man. For this reason, I returned to the church three times to show my appreciation.

ONCE LOST, NOW FOUND

Even though I was still wary about the gospel message and not ready to accept it, I returned to the church one day and asked for prayer. Although I wasn't exactly sure how this prayer thing worked, I had seen it in the church the couple times I had visited and was desperate enough to try. I also respected and trusted the pastor enough to just go with it and see what happened. Upon my request, the pastor invited the entire congregation to lay hands on me and pray for me.

Once they were ready to pray, the pastor asked me to accept Christ as my Lord and Savior. I still did not fully understand the gospel at this point, but I was so impressed with and moved by the pastor's love that I was willing to give it a chance. I could not help but be intrigued by the love that defined the pastor and his congregation. There was no love in my Satanic background. I didn't love my clients like this pastor loved his congregation.

Furthermore, I didn't even love my clients like he loved outsiders. This man, who had only known me a short time, loved me and cared about me deeply. Even more, he attributed the ability to do that to this man named Jesus. Before the prayers started, I decided that this would be the moment that I would accept Christ as my Lord and Savior. As soon as I did this, the demons inside me began screaming and then threw me down on the floor. This, however, was nothing new for the congregation. They had seen this many times and saw the process through to completion. While this experience in the church was certainly one of eternal significance, the true turning point for what daily life looked like followed shortly after my conversion.

VISIONS

One day I fell into what can best be described as a trance. It wasn't a dream because I was not sleeping but a vision. In this trance state, Jesus appeared to me standing in midair about four feet off the ground. When I saw Him, I immediately knew that it was Jesus. When He beckoned me, I saw the scars in His palms. He asked me, "Where are your friends?" I responded, "They are in a nearby trading area doing business." He instructed me twice to go get them. Both times I refused out of fear that Jesus would leave when I left to get them. I wouldn't necessarily say it was a disrespectful refusal. It was more born out of a desire to just be with Jesus.

The third time He asked about my friends, however, my attitude changed, and I became rude. Jesus responded with anger at this refusal and told me again to go get them. Seeing my genuine concern about leaving, Jesus reassured me and said, "I will never leave you nor forsake you." He then said one last time, "Go call your friends and tell them I need them."

Reassured and comforted, I followed His instructions and left to go get my friends. As I left, I came out of the trance. It took some time, prayer, and significant reflection to make sense of what had happened, but reaching the following conclusions brought about a major change in my life.

CALLED BY CONVERSION

I eventually came to understand this visitation from Jesus as a call on my life. There were three important conclusions that I drew as a result, which I will label as people, provision, and ministry. The first was that people had been sent to Africans who otherwise would likely have never heard the gospel. I could see clearly enough in my own life the importance of this. From my friend who invited me to church and shared the gospel with me to the pastor who facilitated my conversion, the importance of people being sent could not be overstated. This led me to the conclusion that clearly people were an essential part of the redemptive equation, and I could sense my role in this area on the verge of significant change.

The second area, the one of provision, was perhaps the most significant in my approaching lifestyle change. The provision aspect centered on the knowledge that God would never leave me nor forsake me. It was easy enough to understand that people had to be sent for others to hear the gospel and that these "others" needed to hear it, but that on its own wouldn't have been enough to make me abandon everything I knew for the sake of the gospel. Significant sacrifice without the full assurance of God's faithfulness would surely be futile. I did not know it at the time, but I would soon find this to be far more true than I originally imagined.

The final part of this realization, the ministry aspect, dealt with evangelism, or the preaching of the gospel to the people of the world. While this call applies to all Christians, this applied to me in a vocational sense. All Christians are called to share the gospel, but not all are called to be pastors of churches. I was being called to be a pastor, which many in Africa would consider to be a figurative death in terms of money and material possessions. Most pastors in Africa have close to nothing in terms of money and material property, but also, as I would soon find out, becoming a pastor could very well lead to a literal, physical death.

chapter four:
starting a church

The church where I was led to Christ warmly welcomed me in the days and months following my conversion. Following up with new Christians is very important, and I was no exception. New converts are often primary targets for Satan and his demons. In many instances, new believers are excited about their faith and eager to tell others about it. This can lead to them being very effective for the kingdom of God. As you know, Satan's main objective is to keep people from Christ; therefore, new Christians tend to pose a significant threat to the kingdom of darkness. This, combined with their lack of experience and often little knowledge of the truth, makes them vulnerable to attack.

To be clear, when one is saved, the Holy Spirit indwells and seals that person, and the eternal protection of God rests on him or her. However, this does not mean that Satan and his demons will not do what they can to hinder one's growth in the faith and effectiveness for the kingdom of God.

Fortunately, the pastor and his congregation knew this and thoroughly followed up with me. The bulk of this dealt with solid biblical teaching. I was taught the design of man, why the need for Christ exists, and the message of salvation. All of these teachings were centered deeply in the Bible. This resonated heavily with me, and once I felt confident enough in my knowledge of the Christian message and ability to communicate it, I began street preaching.

With continued support from the church and practice in communicating this message on the street, I became an effective street preacher. The impromptu questioning that took place during these sessions proved to be valuable training. Seeing the fruit that street preaching brought only increased my hunger for knowledge and experience as a Christian. I began to sense that my role as a Christian was moving toward one of leadership.

This led me to open a home fellowship, which soon grew into a large community church. As the church continued to grow, I realized that more training would be essential if I was to continue pastoring others and preaching the gospel. There were missionaries in a neighboring country who were running a Bible-training school, and I contacted them about enrolling. They welcomed me into the program and quickly realized that I was someone whom God had made highly capable but that the devil had taken advantage of to serve in his kingdom of darkness.

It took me roughly nine months to graduate, and upon graduation I was fully prepared to preach and teach the gospel and did so in the community church I had started. It was not long after this, however, that the call would be taken a step further yet again.

If you think back to the three important realizations I had from the visitation with Jesus Christ, this is one of the times where the provision aspect became so important. Had I any doubt that Jesus would be with me in the impending call on my life, I may not have responded in obedience. God was calling me to go plant a church in another community. He gave me the name of the community, and my initial reaction was not one of submission and trust. Put plainly, I didn't want to go. I didn't want to be a full-time pastor and didn't have any intentions on becoming one, much less one in a new community. From the time of my conversion to this point in my life, ministry and preaching the gospel had been something that I had taken very seriously but not something I considered doing full time.

THE CALL

As I stated earlier, being a pastor in Africa is often synonymous with having very little money. Compensation was not only low; it was often very unpredictable. As many of you probably already know, many parts of Africa are extremely poor, and wherever I would be going was no exception. I also knew that wherever I would be going would likely not have a strong, established Christian presence. This meant that I would have to convince people in an overwhelmingly non-Christian community to come to church and grow a congregation for income to even be a possibility. This was a daunting task to say the least, and bringing this upon my wife and kids seemed almost out of the question.

As a quick aside, since I have now brought them into the story, let me introduce my family. In 1980, shortly after meeting each other, my wife and I moved in together. We had our first child in 1981 and our second in 1983. We officially married in 1984 and are still happily married today. Throughout the course of our years together, we have had seven children, one of whom we lost, and have adopted another twenty-one. My family has been such a tangible representation of the Lord's promise that He would never leave me nor forsake me. While I had reservations about going into the ministry full time, largely due to the fact that I wanted to provide for my family, the Lord ended up using them (my wife in particular) to make vividly clear His call upon my life.

As you can recall, the last time I tried to refuse a direct word from the Lord, He reminded me who was in control. Remembering this, I decided to meet Him halfway and told Jesus that I would only go if my wife agreed. I figured that this was a best-of-both-worlds scenario. I wasn't completely refusing, but I also wasn't saying yes without my wife's approval. Her opinion mattered, and I concluded that if this call to go start a church was something that God truly wanted to me to do, then He would provide a sign in the form of her compliance.

About two weeks later, she came up to me and suggested that we go start a church. I immediately knew that this was the Holy Spirit working in my life and hers, pushing us to abandon fear and trust in Him. During this process, Jesus pointed out to me that He too had suffered. He understood my fear and hesitation, and He reminded me again that He would be with me. He would never leave me nor forsake me, and He made clear that regardless of the problems I faced, I would not fail. With this knowledge and assurance, I committed to following the Lord's call to move and plant a church.

I have come to realize increasingly over the course of my life that God's timing always has a strategic purpose. I see it as no coincidence that I found out I was being sent to a Muslim village after agreeing to follow the Lord's call. When I found this out, deep concern arose within me. It is difficult enough reaching the nonreligious with the gospel, much less those who are already believers in another religion. Not to mention, Islam is deeply rooted in culture and tradition.

For a Muslim, at the very least, leaving the faith often means excommunication from his or her family. It can even mean death for some. How would I reach these people? How would I support my family? Would my family live? All of these questions flooded my mind, and had I not already agreed to follow God's call and been reassured of His devotion to me, I may well have jumped ship.

Regardless of my concern, abandoning my commitment to the Lord was not an option, so we gathered what we had and headed to the Muslim village to start a church. At the time, there were probably around twenty thousand Muslim residents living there. We worked hard to get the church up and running and began by meeting in a borrowed house.

EARLY YEARS OF THE CHURCH

During the first few years, we experienced far more persecution than we did growth. In the first few months, we led four Muslim women to Christ but did not experience much growth past that for the next four years or so. In addition to the difficulty of penetrating the Muslim belief system, persecution became even more intense.

It's not that the gospel message wasn't appealing in and of itself. We found many to be intrigued by the concept of love and union with God. It was everything else that made it tough to gain converts. Imagine being asked to abandon everything your family and those around you have told you is true and valuable since birth. This could include, but is not limited to, career choice, family holidays, and even who you decide to marry. It was undoubtedly a significant sacrifice. Add to that the fact that doing so may lead to additional persecution, or even death, and our message became a difficult sell.

After this four-year period of stagnation, we decided it best to enter a three-day period of consecrated prayer and fasting to ask God why He had sent us into such an unreceptive community. We knew that we had followed Him in obedience, but nothing was happening that seemed to confirm that. What good was it doing for us to struggle financially and experience frequent persecution if we were not seeing any growth in our church? To be clear, it was not about growth for the sake of growth. It was about salvation. It was about people walking out of the same darkness from which I had come and walking into the glorious light of Christ. It was about eternity with God in heaven, an eternity only attained through repentance of sins and faith in Jesus Christ.

During this three-day period of prayer, God answered by giving us two scriptures. The first was Isaiah 45:1–2, which states:

> "Thus says the LORD to His anointed,
> To Cyrus, whose right hand I have held—
> To subdue nations before him
> And loose the armor of kings,
> To open before him the double doors,
> So that the gates will not be shut:
> 'I will go before you
> And make the crooked places straight;
> I will break in pieces the gates of bronze
> And cut the bars of iron."

In short, Cyrus was the Persian king who freed the Jews from a seventy-year period of captivity under the Babylonians. I took this as confirmation that God was going to use me as a vessel to deliver people, but it may take time. It was also a reminder that God uses unlikely people to affect change for His kingdom, even if they can't see it at the time. What made Cyrus unlikely is that he was a pagan, meaning he didn't believe in God, and God still used him to free His people. Regardless of how discouraged, confused, or unqualified I might have felt, this confirmed that God's calling of me to this village was still where He wanted me to be and that He would open doors in His time.

The second scripture was Jeremiah 51:20–24, which states,

> You are My battle-ax and weapons of war:
> For with you I will break the nation in pieces;
> With you I will destroy kingdoms;
> With you I will break in pieces the horse and its rider;
> With you I will break in pieces the chariot and its rider;
> With you also I will break in pieces man and woman;
> With you I will break in pieces old and young;
> With you I will break in pieces the young man and the maiden;
> With you also I will break in pieces the shepherd and his flock;
> With you I will break in pieces the farmer and his yoke of oxen;
> And with you I will break in pieces governors and rulers.
>
> "And I will repay Babylon

And all the inhabitants of Chaldea
For all the evil they have done
In Zion in your sight," says the LORD.

These two scriptures reassured me of God's faithfulness and reaffirmed my belief that I had indeed followed God's call to exactly the place he had for me. I understood this to mean that I was the rightful person sent to minister to this community and that God would use me to deliver His people from the hands of the devil.

With renewed clarity and vigor, I returned to the village excited to see what God would do. However, when I returned I was met with even greater resistance from the Muslim community. Although initially difficult, as any time of persecution is, I felt more grounded and prepared than I had previously. This season of life marked the arrival of a couple more important realizations that would be essential for me as I continued in ministry.

One was that I realized that these experiences were not because I was an inherently special person nor did they make me one. In other words, these struggles were not unique to me because I was any different than anyone else. Everybody struggles. That is the premise of the gospel. Nobody is intrinsically better or more important than anyone else. Everyone is broken by sin and in need of a Savior. I did, however, come to realize that I was likely being called to some unique things by the Lord, and this time of persecution was preparing me for the work ahead that was to be done.

I also had an important spiritual revelation during this time. When we (Christians) pray for anything, the devil and his demons gather their weapons to fight against our progress. Remember that their ultimate goal is to keep people from Jesus, and Christians are the greatest threat on earth to ruining their cause. Because of this, Satan has assigned demons to frustrate Christians and cause their failure. This can come through other people, circumstances, sickness, disease, family problems, etc. I knew, however, from the scriptures received and from personal experience, that God would be faithful.

During this time of trial and persecution, I returned to Jesus's promise from the beginning. He would never leave me nor forsake me. He was my provider and protector and would remain so until He called me home. Because of this, I knew my death would be precious in His eyes, and for this reason I had nothing to fear. I would soon find out, however, that with my newfound security would come an increase in persecution as well.

chapter five:
learning arabic

The turning point for the growth of our church came through another unlikely and unexpected friendship. A radical Muslim man who had been persecuting us decided for some reason that he wanted to become my friend. At the time, I wasn't sure why, but I welcomed the relationship. As we became friends, I grew to respect his knowledge of the Arabic language and his devotion to his religion and the study of the Quran. For these reasons, I asked him to teach me Arabic. While there are other translations of the Quran available, most devout Muslims are taught the Arabic version because it is the language of the original book. They believe that when the Quran is translated it becomes subject to corruption by human error. In other words, they believe that when humans translate the Quran it can be misinterpreted and lose some of its original meaning. So I thought it would be most useful to learn Arabic.

My friend was a little hesitant at first and questioned me about my reasons for wanting to learn. I told him that it was because of his strong faith in Islam, which was true. Also, I told him I wanted to know more about the Quran. I realized that I had been approaching a community of people that was serious about their faith. Most knew the Quran deeply and had had its teaching poured into them since birth. I knew that in order to engage them effectively I had to meet them on their turf, so to speak, so I committed to learning Arabic and the Quran.

Despite my friend's hesitation, he agreed to teach me. He said that he had been praying to Allah and asking him why he had become my friend. He concluded that Allah wanted him to help me become a Muslim, and so he taught me for the next nine months. As a result, I was able to read, write, and speak Arabic by the end of this learning period. I did not, however, become a Muslim. Instead, I started using the Quran to convert Muslims to Christ, which led to significant growth in our church. I introduced them to the Bible by having discussions with them about the Quran and pointing out the Quran's flaws and shortcomings. When they realized how well I knew the Quran, they were much more willing to hear what I had to say regarding the truth of the Bible.

I did not initially approach my teacher once I started using my knowledge of the Quran to reach out to those in the community. I needed some time to prepare myself to speak to him and share the gospel with him. I figured it best to wait a bit. Apparently, I did not wait long enough.

When the time came to approach my friend and former teacher, I did so sharing the gospel and using the Quran to do so. This did not go over well. He became furious and began cursing and yelling, asking me, "Is this the reason you asked me to teach you Arabic?" He was in such a frenzy that it was difficult for me to speak.

The questions then turned into accusations. His voice continuing to rise, he said, "I regret teaching you Arabic! It was a mistake because now you have become a serious threat to Islam!" It was as if hearing the words come out of his mouth made him more angry because the accusations then turned to threats. He said, "I will not rest until your head is mine." He then ran into the house and grabbed a machete, and I ran away as fast as I could.

chapter six:
hand grenade

While somewhat extreme, this is an example of what persecution looked like for me in a Muslim-dominated third-world village. I rested in the fact that God was using this for my good and His glory. Fortunately, this experience with this particular friend was a one-time occurrence, and I was able to continue my ministry to the public.

Once the ministry began gaining some traction, I felt confident enough to engage the Muslim community at large. I decided that figuring out a way to preach to large crowds could be an effective method of outreach. I settled on having an open-air meeting right in the middle of the community. I had already been threatened within an inch of my life, so I had nothing to lose. God had called me to minister to these people, and that's exactly what I intended to do. I wanted to draw as many people as possible, so I put up posters revealing the time and place of the meetings. The crusade would last two weeks, and the goal was to evangelize as many people as possible.

It was very effective. We had somewhere between three and five hundred people that came. Out of those attendees, around one hundred fifty converted from Islam to Christianity. On the last day of the crusade, as usual, I gave an altar call after I finished preaching. For those who may not know what this is, it is the time at the end of a preaching service in which the pastor invites people in the meeting to come up for prayer. While people may certainly come for general prayer, there is often a specific invitation for those ready to accept Christ as their Lord and Savior.

Upon giving the altar call, over fifty people came and gave their life to Christ. It was truly a time of celebration. Before the end of the meeting, I asked the ushers to take the new believers into a bamboo structure for further instruction and prayer. I then invited our praise team to lead us in worship songs. As soon as

I stepped down, a hand grenade exploded in our midst.

I immediately hit the floor from the impact, but I didn't know the extent of my injuries or the injuries of others. I didn't know that my body had been filled with shrapnel or that five children and one man had been killed. What I could sense, though, was that my spirit was beginning to leave my body. I was dying, but I realized in that moment that I wasn't ready to die. I repented of my sins and thought about my wife and children. I wasn't afraid of death, but I couldn't understand why God had brought me this far only to see so little fruit. So I said to the Lord, "Forgive me, but I'm not coming. My children are very young, and I'm not satisfied with what I have contributed toward Your Kingdom. You have invested so much in me, and I still feel that I have more to give. I also have to retaliate against my enemy, the devil. No weapon formed against me shall prosper" (Isaiah 54:17). Immediately, I fell back into my body.

The next thing I knew I was in the hospital. I stayed there for two days before being discharged. The doctors x-rayed my body and saw many pieces of shrapnel, some of which were very close to my heart. During the recovery period, after getting out of the hospital, I reflected heavily on what had happened. I knew God was in control, so fear never entered my mind. I also remembered and rested in Matthew 5:11–12, which states, "Blessed are you when they revile and persecute you, and say all kinds of evil against you falsely for My sake. Rejoice and be exceedingly glad, for great is your reward in heaven, for so they persecuted the prophets who were before you."

I knew that persecution was part of the salvation package (Mark 10:29–30), but knowing that this was a blessing gave me great peace. Knowing that I was called to "rejoice and be exceedingly glad" in the midst of persecution because of the "reward" that was before me gave me an even greater vigor and passion for the ministry. I knew I needed to continue.

While God was deeply instilling these scriptural truths upon my heart, my congregation was hurting. Many were new converts, and they were struggling to understand why this had happened. Some had dealt with personal loss, and nearly all were wondering whether they were next. The new converts, many of whom had made significant sacrifices to follow Christ, were left wondering whether it was really worth it.

chapter seven:
congregational concern

I had just begun to gather a congregation of new believers who were coming to church, being taught the Bible, and engaging in regular fellowship with other believers. This meant that others in the community were beginning to take notice, which is what we wanted. We wanted people to wonder what was so important that we needed to gather on a weekly basis for it. From a ministry standpoint, the hope was that we would experience a snowball effect in reaching people with the gospel, hoping that as we gained a following it would only attract more people.

Whoever threw the hand grenade initially accomplished what they intended, which was the dismantling of the traction we were gaining in leading people to Christ. We posed a threat to the local Muslim culture and their way of life, and they wanted to put an end to it. Without a leader, this may have been accomplished, but God was not done with me, and He had not called me to abandon the people He had given me to lead and disciple. If I abandoned them in the face of persecution, what would that say about the God in whom they had so recently believed? Due to my life experiences, I knew and deeply believed that Jesus would never leave me nor forsake me. Many of the members of the congregation, however, did not.

I knew that people were scared, but fear wasn't my main concern. Fear can come and go and often has the potential to subside with time. What concerned me were the deeper issues that could come as a result of that fear because the fear produced questioning, which can lead to doubting.

To be clear, questioning what you believe is not wrong. However, questioning must be approached with care and caution. When questioning one's beliefs, the Christian is to seek out truth and take this pursuit seriously. Questioning things should be done with the intent of returning to Christ and remaining in truth. When one approaches the act of questioning out of fear or with an attitude of nonchalance, the consequences can be dangerous. It is in these times that Satan is given a foothold to turn questioning into doubt.

For example, we see the effect of a nonchalant attitude toward discernment in Genesis 3. Consequently, this nonchalance forever changed the world. Consider Genesis 3:1–7:

> Now the serpent was more cunning than any beast of the field which the LORD God had made. And he said to the woman, "Has God indeed said, 'You shall not eat of every tree of the garden'?"
>
> And the woman said to the serpent, "We may eat the fruit of the trees of the garden; but of the fruit of the tree which is in the midst of the garden, God has said, 'You shall not eat it, nor shall you touch it, lest you die.'"
>
> Then the serpent said to the woman, "You will not surely die. For God knows that in the day you eat of it your eyes will be opened, and you will be like God, knowing good and evil."
>
> So when the woman saw that the tree was good for food, that it was pleasant to the eyes, and a tree desirable to make one wise, she took of its fruit and ate. She also gave to her husband with her, and he ate. Then the eyes of both of them were opened, and they knew that they were naked; and they sewed fig leaves together and made themselves coverings.

If you are not familiar with this passage, this was the moment that sin came into the world. This was the moment that humankind surrendered their God-given dominion over the earth-world to Satan. This forever changed the condition of the world. Satan took advantage of the nonchalant attitude of Eve and used it to deceive her.

While nonchalance was not as much the case with the people of my congregation, it's nonetheless important to be aware of when approaching the act of questioning. The large majority of my congregation fell into the mindset driven by fear. While fear can be a natural response to things that happen to us, it is not something to which we should submit and certainly not a state in which we should stay. The Bible makes this clear in 2 Timothy 1:7, stating, "For God has not given us a spirit of fear, but of power and of love and of a sound mind." Satan, however, does all that he can to disrupt this spirit that God has given His children. Consider Peter's denial of Jesus in Mark 14:66–72:

> Now as Peter was below in the courtyard, one of the servant girls of the high priest came. And when she saw Peter warming himself, she looked at him and said, "You also were with Jesus of Nazareth."
>
> But he denied it, saying, "I neither know nor understand what you are saying." And he went out on the porch, and a rooster crowed.
>
> And the servant girl saw him again, and began to say to those who stood by, "This is one of them." But he denied it again.
>
> And a little later those who stood by said to Peter again, "Surely you are one of them; for you are a Galilean, and your speech shows it."
>
> Then he began to curse and swear, "I do not know this Man of whom you speak!"
>
> A second time the rooster crowed. Then Peter called to mind the word that Jesus had said to him, "Before the rooster crows twice, you will deny Me three times." And when he thought about it, he wept.

Here, Peter, one of Jesus's disciples, is seized by a moment of fear and denies any association he has with Jesus. This was a man who had spent significant time with Jesus, followed Jesus, been taught by Jesus, and even underwent a name change from Simon to Peter upon becoming a disciple (John 1:42). Additionally, when Jesus predicts Peter's denial in verse 30 of the same chapter, Peter responds in verse 31 by saying, "If I have to die with You, I will not deny You!" (Mark 14:31). In other words, Peter says that he would die before he denied Jesus, and yet, he denied Jesus not once but three times due to fear.

If Peter could deny Jesus in a time of fear, then what would become of my congregation? They didn't have the background that Peter did. Many were new believers and had just watched people die for no other reason than the fact that they were at a Christian gathering.

I knew that they would be easy targets for Satan. He could use this fear to draw them into questioning and turn the questioning into doubt. Doubt can make people very ineffective, and I knew that Satan did not want these new believers to be effective in living for God and spreading the gospel.

I could all but hear the questions I imagined were swirling around in their heads. Is this going to happen to me next? Have I been targeted because somebody saw me at the meeting? Will my family be safe? All of these were natural responses to what had happened; however, natural doesn't always mean appropriate. The deeper questions born out of these were what concerned me. These are what I consider to be the "if" questions. These are questions that come about as a result of something else. An "if" question, in this situation, might look something like this: "If God allowed this to happen, does this mean He doesn't love us?" Or "If this happened, does this mean God doesn't exist?" Or even, "Since this happened, does that mean that the powers of darkness are greater than the powers of God?"

These were the questions that could lead to doubt, and if there was not a solid leader who was confident in the promises of God, then this would likely happen. I simply could not stand by idly. I knew that God was calling me to return and be that leader. The spiritual battle was imminent, and I was ready to engage in the fight. As the healing process came to a close, I returned to the village from which I had so recently been removed.

chapter eight:
rebuilding the church

The concerns that I had were quickly confirmed. People were scared not only to go to church but also to even identify as Christians. I knew that I had to lead by example, and this involved two main things: preaching the gospel and spending time with people. These are two things that Jesus did a lot of during His time on earth. He was dedicated to preaching truth and valued spending time with people. He invested particularly in His disciples, knowing that they would play a very significant role in the foundation and growth of the church after He ascended into heaven. I knew that one of my primary duties as a pastor was to disciple my congregation. This meant encouraging them, challenging them, and teaching them what it means to be a follower of Christ.

Now, take a moment and imagine yourself in the position of one of my new converts. You have recently believed upon a message centered on the inherent goodness of God. In short, this message states that God, in His goodness, loves us so much that He left heaven in the form of His Son Jesus Christ to proclaim the message of salvation, died a terrible and tortuous death for this proclamation, and rose from the grave three days later to eternally defeat sin and death once and for all. His death paid for the sins of man and made possible the forgiveness of those sins for all who believe. This is indeed good news!

Particularly for the Islamic community was this good news. I will expound on this later in the book, but the message of Islam does not portray a loving god that deeply desires fellowship with those he has created. Instead, it gives us a god that humans are incapable of relationship with and must work to please. Additionally, there is no guarantee of an eternal afterlife free from the pain and sorrow of this world nor one spent in the presence of God Himself. For the Christian, this guarantee is because the God who created us, loves us, and wants to be with us invites us into His presence. There was much appeal to this message to those in the community, but, like most things, appeal only remains a good thing if it proves to be true. If God was indeed as good as the gospel proclaimed, then why had innocent people died for believing in this message?

My task was to remind and show the people of my congregation that this message of God's goodness was indeed true and would remain to be true regardless of the persecution that might come. This was where the value of my in-depth Bible training took on a new level of importance. Christianity, particularly in America, tends to be comfortable and feel-good until people are met with serious adversity and have little or no theological foundation. Theology, in short, is the study of God and His relation to the world. This can range from topics with answers easier to understand such as why God sent His Son Jesus Christ to die for the sins of man, to more complicated issues such as the origin of God or why He allowed evil into the world in the first place. While theological depth does not dictate salvation, having a solid foundation is important, and this foundation often grows the more you progress in your relationship with the Lord.

Like any relationship, people grow in knowledge and in trust of one another the more they know about the other person. For example, let's say that you have a good friend who is notoriously bad at returning phone calls. If you did not know them well, you would likely assume that they didn't care for you very much or didn't have much interest in talking to you. However, because you have spent a lot of time getting to know them, you know that when they don't return your calls it is because they are either busy or simply forgot. It is not because they are mad at you or don't like you. It's just part of who they are, and you grow to trust them in that.

Much of the same can be said about the ways in which we view God and relate to Him. To be clear, God is not a God who is ever too busy for us, and He does not neglect us when we call upon Him. Things, however, happen that we may not understand or even like, but the more we know about Him, the more likely we are to trust Him. Most of my congregation was lacking in the theological category so this would be a big part of my ministry to them going forward.

The other significant aspect of my ministry would simply be being consistent. My faith in Christ and my following of His call to go plant a church hinged on the fact that Jesus told me He would never leave me nor forsake me. This was the very essence of consistency. I knew that if I was to model my life after Christ's, then consistently showing up to minister to my congregation was nonnegotiable.

I began by visiting their homes. I also spent the entire month preaching on love and persecution. Mark 10:28–30 served as the foundation of my message:

> Then Peter began to say to Him, "See, we have left all and followed You."
>
> So Jesus answered and said, "Assuredly, I say to you, there is no one who has left house or brothers or sisters or father or mother or wife or children or lands, for My sake and the gospel's, who shall not receive a hundredfold now in this time—houses and brothers and sisters and mothers and children and lands, with persecutions—and in the age to come, eternal life.

The message here is clear. Persecution is part of our Christian life, but not only that, it is a blessing because of its eternal significance for the believer.

Matthew also refers to the "prophets" of old (Matt. 5:12). One important takeaway from this reference is the fact that the persecution of Christians is nothing new. In regards to our situation, God was not in heaven wringing His hands wondering why this happened to His poor believers. No, this was certainly nothing new, and God was certainly still sovereign. Instead, it was a call for the believer to lean more heavily into Christ and trust His plan and His faithfulness. Just as He had ultimately delivered the prophets and rewarded them in heaven, so too would He deliver and reward those who endured this time of persecution in my village.

What this means, not just for those in my village but for all passionate, born-again believers is that persecution will inevitably come. It may not come in the form of a hand grenade nearly taking your life, but it will come in some form or another. Remember, however, as I reminded my congregation, that persecution does not come without purpose. Jesus's instruction to "rejoice and be exceedingly glad" in Matthew 5:12 indicates that greater things are coming, which is not only assurance of the purpose in persecution but also the affirmation of the love God has for His people.

Slowly but surely, through the preaching of this message and the faithfulness of God, the church regained its membership. By the end of my first month back, we had gone from zero members to around one hundred, and God was just getting started.

SECTION TWO

present day

chapter nine:
impact of the church

God's promises have proven to be true. He didn't leave me. He didn't forsake me. In fact, it has been quite the opposite. God has poured His blessing out on our ministry and grown the small community church that we started into a thriving network of churches throughout Africa. He has provided long-standing partners who have assisted not only financially but have also helped create sustainable business models that encourage and support community growth. Most importantly, all of this translates into souls won for the Kingdom of God.

I want to be clear in that what follows in this chapter is in no way intended to be a boast of what we have accomplished. It is more intended to highlight what can happen when we wholly submit ourselves to following God's will and prioritize looking to the Holy Spirit for guidance in our lives. God saved me and called me to this kingdom work. I am just His vessel, striving to follow His call on my life. It's not about the buildings or number of churches that we have. It's not about starting something from the ground up with little idea of what we were doing or how it would be accomplished. It's not about the amount of money that has been donated to support the ministry. It's about the fact that God is drawing people to Himself and choosing to allow us to be a part of what He is doing. We recognize that our role is to trust Him and live in obedience to His call.

I also want to highlight some of the differences in the Western church model and the Eastern church model. While there are certainly exceptions to the rule, I have observed patterns and trends over the years in my time spent in Africa and America. Many times, in Western nations, churches are largely modeled after Western corporations. They are guided and controlled by man-made objectives, plans, reports, forms, etc. In many ways, this makes sense. In America, arguably the most advanced country in the world, the concept of success is heavily tied to the corporate model. Success is found in the most efficient, effective, and productive models that man can create. So it makes sense that the natural inclination of those in the church would be to reflect this mentality.

In many instances, the intent is good. People are using their best efforts to accomplish what they believe God wants. However, this model can lead people to relying on personal wisdom rather than the guidance of the Holy Spirit. I see this method as one that is certain to fail. I have seen in my life that I cannot successfully guide myself in working for the Lord. I must wait on the Holy Spirit and rely on Him for guidance. It is the ability to wait that seems to have been largely lost in the Western Church. In my view, our actions and answers are worthless unless we wait on Him.

The statistics and models in this chapter are intended to promote deeper consideration of what it looks like to approach ministry with the guidance of the Holy Spirit. Financial support is a central part of facilitating church and Kingdom growth. It is my hope that you will use the information in this chapter to consider what it looks like to most effectively use your resources for the glory of God.

CURRENT STATE OF THE CHURCH (2018)

The church was founded in 1992 with four members and no assets. Today, we have approximately 220 churches located throughout our country. The average membership for each church is around 220, which equates to a total membership of approximately fifty thousand. God is continuing to move in powerful ways, and we expect the ministry to continue to grow. The following growth projections are based on current trends regarding the establishment of new branches.

I want to note here that the following projections are spiritual in nature. What I mean by this is that they are inspired and accomplished by the Holy Spirit. I understand that when viewed from a business-oriented standpoint these numbers may seem a bit unrealistic and ambitious. Most businesses, corporations, and churches do not experience exponential growth on a continually-consistent basis. There will be good years, down years, and often times, eventually a point where rapid and exponential expansion no longer becomes realistic due to a variety of factors (competition, limited resources, cost/benefit of expansion, etc.).

We credit our growth to the working of the Holy Spirit and base our projections off what we have seen and experienced thus far. When the pastors that we train become filled with the Holy Spirit, they experience a profound desire to share the gospel with the masses. Our pastors are genuinely hungry to see as many people as possible come to salvation in Christ. This combined with our "branch church" model has led to exponential growth in our church. As we continue to train and send pastors out to plant churches, growth continues to occur. Each branch church is taught and expected to plant a new branch each year. As long as the Lord sees fit for this to continue, rapid growth and expansion is inevitable. The plans of the Lord and the fire of the Holy Spirit simply cannot be stopped.

I have chosen to include the following projections to highlight these spiritually-empowered growth rates. God has already done far more than we could have imagined; therefore, we see no reason to put limitations on what He will do in the future.

YEAR	NUMBER OF BRANCHES	AVERAGE MEMBERSHIP	EST. TOTAL MEMBERSHIP (by end of year)
2018	220	220 people	48,400 people
2019	320	242 people	77,440 people
2020	420	266 people	111,720 people
2021	520	293 people	167,010 people
2022	570	322 people	183,540 people

Each time a new church is planted, it transforms the village it occupies. This happens both economically and spiritually. Many of the areas where we plant churches are severely poverty-stricken. People are living in desperate conditions, and there is often little to no strong Christian presence in these communities.

With poverty comes a complete lack of sustainable and profitable economic growth. Trade skills are often low because, even if goods were produced, many people wouldn't have the money to buy them. What little money is made is often spent on food. It is a desperate cycle that has afflicted many of these communities for generations. We knew that one of our responsibilities as a church was to help however we could economically; we just didn't know how we would do that.

THE MODEL

Around 2002, God provided the people who would help us grow the church from humble beginnings to a thriving network. These people were businessmen from America who came not only with financial resources but also business models to put these resources to work. These American partners were people who, although from vastly different cultural and economic backgrounds, shared the same passion as I did for advancing the Kingdom of God. These models were designed to not only bring revenue to the church and the community but also to empower the people occupying these areas.

These American partners, who quickly became close friends, and I discussed what might be most effective. It was apparent that they were both eager to help and in it for the long haul. They did not want to just throw money at the problem and call it a day. They wanted to know what the needs were and formulate a plan to best meet them.

After much discussion and prayer, we felt that the Holy Spirit was guiding us to sustainable agriculture. Several reasons came to mind. For one, the skills needed to sustain these practices are relatively easy to learn. Tending to animals and the land would primarily require people who were willing to work, and we had people willing to work. Another reason was that there was opportunity for natural growth without continued capital investment. For example, animals are able to breed naturally. This produces more animals that you do not have to purchase. More animals lead to more product, which often leads to more profit. Another benefit of the agricultural model was the food it would provide for the people of the communities. We often sell it, but we also will donate it depending on the need. Regardless of whether we sell or donate, the intent is always to pour what we reap back into the community. Lastly, certain areas of agriculture provide a relatively quick return on investment. For example, some chickens in their prime can lay anywhere from one to six eggs per week, which can immediately be used for nourishment or sale.

In addition to the practicality of sustainable agriculture, we also decided this would be a worthwhile endeavor since I had extensive experience raising chickens. If you think back to the early days of my church—the first four years where the first four women who joined were our only members—I had to find a way to generate income to provide for my family, so I began raising chickens. The reasons I decided on this were the same as I just mentioned: low cost of entry and ongoing profit if done correctly.

During that time, I was not receiving any capital from outside sources. This meant that I had to really hone in on becoming the best and most efficient chicken farmer that I could be. This was, perhaps, the beginning of my relationship with the concept of stewardship and also the beginning of my soon-to-be chicken farming expertise. In order to be the best chicken farmer possible, I had to grow the best chickens I could grow. So I devoted myself to learning all that I could about growing chickens.

This led me to focus on one primary area of production: nutrition. I knew that optimal nutrition often leads to optimal growth and development in humans. Chickens, I thought, should be no different. I learned that optimal growth was achieved by certain combinations of macronutrients (protein, fat, carbohydrates) and micronutrients (vitamins and minerals). Based upon this knowledge, I began developing a formula for my own chicken feed that would facilitate maximum growth. It was a mutually beneficial process and product for all involved.

It was beneficial to me for several reasons. It significantly increased my knowledge of raising chickens, it was much more cost effective than buying feed from someone else, and in the end, it grew bigger and healthier chickens than the average feed that I could purchase would. Bigger and healthier chickens meant more product, which meant more profit. It was beneficial for the chickens because it was a natural and healthy way of raising them. As for the other animals involved in the feed-making process, I considered my use of the parts not normally used for food as part of being a steward of what God had given me. Nothing went to waste.

After some trial and error, I developed the following formula:

1. Maize (corn) bran: This covered the carbohydrate component of the feed. Maize is a starch, and starch is a form of carbohydrate.

2. Cotton cakes: These covered the fat component of the feed. They were made from the leftover cotton seeds once they had been pressed for oil.

3. Roasted soy: This made up the plant protein portion of the formula.

4. Crushed fish: This made up the animal protein portion of the feed.

5. Dried cattle blood: This was used to add calcium (micronutrient) to the feed.

6. The ashes of burnt cattle bones: The ashes provided iron.

7. Salt: This served to provide sodium and potassium.

These seven components provided everything needed to grow strong, healthy chickens. Although sometimes a bit unorthodox, the process for acquiring these products was often relatively easy and inexpensive.

Gathering the fish was by far the most unique part of the process. To harvest these tiny fish, which were about two inches in length, we would take our boat far out into the lake late at night with lanterns in tow. Once we reached the location of the fish, we would turn the lanterns on to activate the harvest. The bright light would cause the fish to jump out of the water and into the boat. On a normal night, the boat would fill up in about thirty minutes. If we stayed with the lights on much longer than thirty minutes, we risked overfilling the boat, which would have caused it to sink. Looking back, there were probably a few times that we should have sunk. Catching these fish, however, was part of the bigger picture that God was piecing together, and His hand of protection was upon us even in this. At the time, those late nights on the lake were spent with the main intention of providing for my family. Little did I know that years down the road God would use my experience raising chickens to serve as the cornerstone of a sustainable agricultural model that would help grow our church family. With raising chickens as the foundation of our model, we explored and prayed about other agricultural projects we could focus on as well.

Through further discussion and prayer, the Holy Spirit led us to focus on four primary areas of production: poultry, fish, trees, and coffee. We chose poultry and fish as our primary food investments. Some of the trees, particularly mango, we also use for food. The coffee, although not a necessity, has proven a valuable area of investment. The eucalyptus trees, the majority of our tree production, was a long-term investment. We would let them sit over time and then experience a large yield when it came time to harvest.

ROLE OF THE BUSINESSMEN

Once the business plans were established, we began working to get them up and running. The American partners provided the capital needed to get started, with the goal that once everything was in place and functioning, we would take over from there. Our investors wanted to help us create a self-sustaining church model that would grow by us owning the income-producing assets and reinvesting all net cash flows in expanding the whole church organization. The importance of this relational dynamic with the businessmen cannot go overstated. The Americans would provide the initial capital for a specific endeavor, but that would be it. This money would be a one-time gift. If we failed, there would not be another sum of money given to attempt that same business endeavor. It may sound a bit harsh, but it was also an investment that they would never ask to be repaid, regardless of whether we were successful or not. We approached it this way because we believed, on both sides, that this was a necessary component of proper stewardship.

For the Americans, continually investing money in a situation where it wasn't used wisely would be poor stewardship. For those of us in Africa, to squander those gifts would be poor stewardship. The stakes were high, but they had to be. We realized that this was a once in a lifetime opportunity. The people of my community needed to be empowered, and part of being empowered is being responsible for things entrusted to one's personal care. We recognized the Americans' generosity as a blessing and gift from God, and we did not intend to waste it.

FROM START-UP TO SELF-SUSTAINING

Let's look at what it took to start our chicken operation. The first thing we needed was land. Once we purchased the land, we built sturdy chicken coops, starting with one and adding on as needed. These chicken coops looked more like prisons than chicken houses. They were made out of bricks, had bars on the windows, and were designed more to keep thieves out than to house chickens. We then selected and trained people to conduct the chicken operation. Once the appropriate people were in place, we bought small chicks and enough feed for five months. The chicks grew into chickens and eventually began laying eggs, which led to a constant supply. Once we consistently started having enough eggs, we began selling them and establishing customers in nearby communities. The sale of eggs and meat (when the chickens stopped routinely producing eggs) initiated the cash flow, which eventually exceeded the expenses needed to start the operation. This took about a year, and at the end of that first year, we were considered self-sustaining. It was at this point that we were expected to begin using the internally-generated resources to expand our ministry.

The initial capital investment for this operation was around $60,000. Once we surpassed the break-even level, the chicken business paid for all its ongoing costs and generated money for expansion. Since achieving the original break-even level, the chicken business has generated roughly $14,000 per year in egg and meat net cash flow since 2006. This means that the chicken business has enabled the church to invest around $168,000 in expansion work to date. We expect this level of cash generation to continue indefinitely (sixty-year asset life) since all the construction is of permanent design. This means that the chicken business alone will generate an estimated $840,000 over the course of its expected life.

The American businessmen helped us with numbers and projections of where we would like to be in the years to come, but we were (and still are) the ones running the day-to-day operations. As stewards of the resources God has given us, we wanted (and still want) to use the resources to reach as many people as possible. Sustaining the business after the initial investment from the Americans allowed future resources to be used to engage new communities. In other words, instead of continually putting money into the same village, we used that same money to start new projects in new areas.

We knew that the success of these endeavors would cause a stir in the communities, so we took things seriously. Our hope was that our operations would move people from malnutrition to health, from unemployed to employed, and most importantly, from nonbelievers to children of God. We wanted people to ask questions. We wanted them to see the church as a place of nourishment, not just physically but, more importantly, spiritually. We wanted to demonstrate through our church-oriented business operations that we loved the communities that we were in, and even greater than that, that God loved them. Our hope was that through these activities, people outside the family of God would see the church as a place of refuge, truth, and love. We entrusted all of this to God and placed it in His hands, and as always, He has been faithful to bless us and walk alongside us every step of the journey.

TODAY

Today, we have about fifteen thousand chickens, four fish ponds with roughly ten thousand fish each, twelve thousand mango trees, sixty thousand eucalyptus trees, and several acres of coffee plants. These operations provide employment, revenue, and opportunities for ministry in the communities that we serve. Although we have branch churches in various locations in our country, most of these operations exist relatively close to our main church. All the revenue that is generated comes to the main church. We then use it to meet the needs of our main location, our branch churches, and to build new branches.

All the profits made go to continuing and expanding our ministry efforts. Whether it is paying for children's school fees, food, clothing, salaries for church staff, or buildings for new churches, we use the money in ways that the Holy Spirit leads us to further the Kingdom of our God. His blessing on these activities enables our ministry to continue to grow. It has, for the most part, allowed us to be accepted when we move into a new area. As you know, when Christians move into new areas to plant churches in Africa, they don't always receive a warm welcome. Through these businesses, however, our church has created jobs, related training, community development, and personal empowerment that has led to a positive outlook in the communities that we serve.

As a result, the church and its leaders are highly respected, which has caused us to be more effective and more influential in reaching out to local communities with discipleship. As you will see in the next chapter, the mentality of people living in places such as Africa is often far different than the mentality of people living in places such as America. Still, God has used our efforts to build an avenue of trust and break down the preconceived barriers that challenge most Christian ministries.

ADDING TO THE KINGDOM

At the end of the day, this translates to souls saved for the Kingdom of God. Paying careful attention to the ways in which we generate and spend our money has allowed us to continue to expand our ministry, and we take this stewardship seriously. We do not focus on having state-of-the-art facilities with cutting-edge technology; we focus on expanding to new areas to reach people who desperately need to know the love and salvation of Jesus Christ. With that being said, we have developed some estimates to represent the cost of adding someone to the Kingdom of God in Africa versus America.

On average, we have received roughly $60,000 per year from our American partners to invest in new businesses and areas of ministry. Like the chicken project, this yearly capital is a one-time investment intended to go toward a specific new venture for the growth of our ministry. This has been ongoing for the last fifteen years, which means there has been a total of approximately $900,000 in total outside investment for our ministry activities. Each new project is projected to have around a sixty-year life cycle. The structures are simple and made from steel, bricks, sheet metal, etc., so they are designed to be sturdy and not require expensive repair.

From 2002 to 2017, we generated an average net cash flow of $50,000 per year. This combines to give us a total cash flow of approximately $750,000 over the past fifteen years. The following is how we determined the cost of adding a soul to the Kingdom:

- Cash Cost (capital plus cash flow)
  - $900,000 + $750,000 = $1,650,000
  - $1,650,000/50,000 = $33.00 per soul added to the Kingdom

- Adjusted Cost (capital consumed plus cash flow)
  - $16.25 per soul added
- Net Cost per Soul per Dollar of Foreign Investment
  - $4.50 per soul added to the Kingdom
  - Note that $15.00 (77%) of the true net cost per soul came from money generated by the local church

In America, the estimates were vastly different. It was estimated that a church with 5,000 members, on average, spends anywhere from $200,000 to $1,000,000 per year on evangelism. We'll use these two numbers for calculation's sake. It was also estimated that the average number of new souls added to the Kingdom (excluding transfers from other churches) through each church's evangelistic work was around 200. Using the same formula as in the third-world church model, here are the following calculations:

- $200,000/200 = $1,000 per individual
- $1,000,000/200 = $5,000 per individual

These estimates are averages and do not reflect specific or individual churches. I did, however, provide them because I think they might serve as useful illustrations and help in thinking about how to most effectively use our resources for the Kingdom. To be clear, we are not intending to portray salvation in a corporate light. In other words, it is not about numbers for the sake of numbers. It is about individuals experiencing the life-changing power of a relationship with Jesus Christ. God cares just as much about the soul saved in Africa as He does about the soul saved in America or anywhere else. However, as stewards of the resources God has given us, we are called to use them as wisely as possible.

This does not mean that you should stop supporting your local church and strictly send money to Africa or another third-world country. Supporting the local church is very important. It does mean, however, that we should be mindful of where our money is going and whether it is being used effectively for the Kingdom of God. In America, many do not consider this because money is often plentiful. Many Americans may not know where their money goes once they tithe it to the church. In Africa, however, we see this money, whether donated or generated, as a blessing and gift from God and know we must use it in the best way possible. It is my prayer that we all consider how to best use our resources to support ministry activities that expand the Kingdom of God here on the earth.

chapter ten:
east vs. west

If you look at the geographic prominence of the major religions in the world, you will likely notice a trend. That trend is that the major world religions (Christianity, Islam, Hinduism, and Buddhism) have tended to stay confined to the general areas in which they originated. Christianity, however, is an exception. If you look at a world map of majority religion by country, you will see this to be true. Hinduism and Buddhism both have roots in India and have largely remained within that region in terms of their spread of influence. Islam, while experiencing quite a larger spread of influence than Hinduism and Buddhism, still pales in comparison to the spread of Christianity. Islam's majority influence, for the most part, has branched out from its origins in the Arabian Peninsula and remained in the Middle East. Christianity, however, while also originating in the Middle East (Jerusalem), has spread to become the majority religion of North America, South America, Australia, most of Europe, and about half of Africa. Consider this map detailing majority religion by country:

For a color version, please visit http://d3tt741pwxqwm0.cloudfront.net/WGBH/sj14/sj14-int-religmap/index.html

Christianity gravitates toward desperate areas. In areas of greatest desperation, the gospel message of salvation makes its greatest impact. In recent decades, Christianity has moved from its original expansion to Europe and America to the Southern Hemisphere. In South America and Africa, we find many countries that are far less developed than the rest of the world, particularly the United States. In these less-developed countries, poverty is rampant and people are desperate. The hope that the gospel message offers, the desperation of the people, and the Christian's call in Matthew 28 to "go…and make disciples of all the nations" combine to facilitate this rapid expansion. The fact that Christianity is growing in these parts of the world is due in large part to the stark differences that exist between Eastern countries and Western ones. To be clear, I'm using the term "Eastern" to describe these underdeveloped countries. This is because the primary focus is Africa and parts of the Middle East/Asia, which classify as being in the East. Although I use the term "Western" to primarily represent America, this term also represents the more developed countries of Europe, Canada, etc. These differences produce very different manifestations of the Christian faith.

As you will see in this chapter, the ways in which Christianity spreads and thrives tends to be directly tied to the economic and spiritual climates of an area. In short, when Christianity invades one of these third-world countries and gains momentum, the response and following thereafter tends to be quite passionate and dedicated. In the developed countries of the West, however, there is little notion of spiritual revival, and the religious climate tends to be more cultural than passionate.

MENTALITY OF DESPERATION

When intense poverty exists on an epidemic level, it extends to every area of the life of the one affected. It is not merely about money. It's about access to conveniences of modern society, personal and family safety, expectations for one's life, and one's view of his or her self-worth. In places where widespread poverty is severe, access to modern conveniences such as medicine or running water, or even education, is difficult to obtain at best. Safety is compromised simply because desperate people are more likely to do desperate things. Fueling the desperation is the attitude that things are not likely to change.

All of this combines to strip away the dignity of personhood. Regardless of how people feel about themselves, there will always be a desire for self-worth. This is because we are created in the image of God, and He assigns us worth.

However, because of the broken condition of the world and our inherent brokenness as humans, many are blinded to the self-worth that we have just through being created by God alone.

This means that if one of our greatest desires as humans is to attain a concept of self-worth, then we will constantly seek out things that we think will accomplish this for us. This is true for all people. It's why those who are wealthy tend to live in nice houses and drive nice cars. It's also why gang culture tends to be far more prevalent in impoverished communities. Both are ways of attaching oneself to something and thereby creating a personal identity. These identities, however, are only a façade. They do not satisfy on a soul-level, and those who seek identity and self-worth through these pursuits are still left searching at the end of the day.

What makes the search for identity different for the one living in desperation is that it's harder to acquire things that distract one from the pursuit of God. In the West, it is very easy to acquire things that temporarily mask the need for God. For example, when someone gets sick in the United States, it is generally easy for him or her to obtain access to a doctor or hospital and get the care that they need to get better. Whether it is medication or surgery or tests to diagnose a problem, even the poorest in America have readily available access to these resources and services. Think about how this shapes the mentality regarding God, who is the ultimate healer. Most of the time when people who have access to these resources get sick the first thought is seeing a doctor to get help. This is because there is a trust that doctors and modern medicine will be able to heal the issue. To be clear, doctors and modern medicine are not bad things; they just tend to be the first line of defense when something goes wrong medically. People's first thought when sick in the West is not generally to call upon the Lord (or any other believed deity) for healing.

Now imagine how the mentality might be different if access to these resources was not readily available. Many in third-world countries depend on herbs, roots, teas, etc. (natural sources) for healing, which prove to not be a very reliable source of medical care. This fuels the desperation mentality. Simple issues, such as infections, that many in the West do not normally consider very serious can be fatal in the East. When those in affluent countries get an infection of some sort, there are antibiotics that are often quite effective at treating the bacteria causing the infection. If those in affluent countries did not have access to these medications, then there would likely be much more fear and uncertainty regarding these issues.

What I'm getting at is that one of the defining characteristics of a desperate mentality is a general lack of assurance in life. There is little assurance of having enough food to feed one's family, having consistent and profitable employment, having a safe and solid structure in which to live, and having access to modern medical care and education. While the gospel message provides no guarantees that all of life's problems will be solved and all material wants will be taken care of when one accepts Christ, it does provide the assurance of provision and eternal life free from the ills that plague the world in which we currently live. A relationship with Jesus Christ provides acceptance into God's kingdom, eternal love, forgiveness, provision, and a process of life-transformation that begins the moment one accepts Christ as Lord and Savior of his or her life. This is why the gospel message is particularly powerful to those who live in desperation. They are looking for change and assurance. They are looking for something outside of themselves that guarantees provision. When met with the message of salvation, there is often already a great desire for immediate change. When they realize that Christ provides this, they take this seriously and are often very passionate and dedicated followers of Christ as a result. They want to obey God and want to tell others about the hope they've found; thus, Christianity begins to thrive in these areas.

THE MESSAGE OF RELIGION

While Christianity is clearly the most powerful, as evidenced by the map of religious spread, other religions are still a powerful tool of the enemy to deceive and keep people from Christ. Although Christianity tends to thrive in these desperate areas, that is not always the case and is certainly not an overnight process. The deception lies in what I will call the "message of religion." This message entails the notion that there is something greater than we are that gives us the ability to transcend our circumstances and find purpose outside of ourselves.

The reason these deceptive messages are appealing goes back to what I said in chapter 1 about our desire for control. They give people an outlet for achieving purpose and perceived self-control; however, there is no love within this mode of operation. This is why Christianity proves to be so powerful in these areas. Most who seek identity and fulfilment in these areas, even if they do not admit it, eventually reach a point where they realize that even their greatest efforts fail them. This is in large part why the Christian message is so powerfully infiltrating these Muslim communities. If everything was right and okay with their attempts at being a good Muslim, then the message of Christianity would likely have no appeal. However, the message that God loves us in spite of our shortcomings and even our best failed attempts at being our own savior is undeniably appealing.

One thing that is characteristically true of humanity is that things tend to work in cycles. Businesses go through periods of growth and decline, sports teams have good years and bad years, and people have times of health and times of sickness. This cyclical nature is also true regarding how we tend to operate as humans. What I mean by this is that bad decisions tend to beget bad decisions, and good decisions tend to beget good decisions. This is not to say that once a bad decision is made that one is incapable of making a good decision, but often the point of change comes in the midst of a pattern of bad decisions. This is what makes us realize we need to change. It's not that we make one mistake but that our mistakes have compounded into a lifestyle. This is because our decisions affect our psyche and the ways in which we view ourselves. This all cycles back to our desire for control. When we make a harmful decision, although it may feel good in the moment, we inevitably realize that it won't satisfy and are left wondering why we did it in the first place. Ultimately, there is some level of realization, even if subconscious, that we aren't in control of ourselves as much as we thought. This leads to shame, and shame is not a comfortable emotion. In order to escape this feeling of shame, we seek pleasure. Sinful (harmful) decisions bring momentary pleasure, and this becomes the easiest outlet to attain that escape from shame. These decisions inevitably compound until we are met with the reality that things need to change.

The same can be said about good decisions. While more difficult to make because of our sinful nature, good decisions build our self-esteem and restore our worth. One reason for this is that good decisions often lead to good consequences, and we have been created to thrive in the presence of good consequences.

The general message of religion caters to this inherent truth of how we operate as humans. Religions provide a blueprint for how we can right our wrongs: how we can free ourselves from guilt, how we can improve our decision making, how we can live a more peaceful and fulfilling life on earth, and in many cases, what we can expect after death. This can make it difficult for Christianity to take root in the communities that we target. Many people are already on a religious trajectory that they believe is right. These beliefs are often rooted deeply in their history as a people group and have great cultural significance.

The message of Christianity, however, presents a unique alternative to their belief system, and that is the fact that our efforts are not what save us. It is the life, death, and resurrection of Jesus Christ and our faith in Him that saves. Even though their belief systems may be deeply rooted, many still experience a life lived with the Eastern mindset. This means that they are still desperate, still seeking, and still lacking a sense of assurance in life. While it may be difficult to initially enter these communities and present the gospel in a convincing manner, the message is still undeniably appealing. When this appeal begins to convince, however, lives are changed, communities are transformed, and the Eastern mentality of religious deception and desperation is turned into a Christlike mentality of hope, forgiveness, and assurance.

chapter eleven:
islam

While there are many, perhaps the biggest threat facing Christianity today is the rise and prominence of Islam. It sits right behind Christianity as the largest religion in the world, with about 1.3 billion adherents. All religions other than Christianity are Satanic deceptions created to distract and draw people away from Christ. So this makes Islam the greatest spiritual threat facing the world at large. In addition to the spiritual element, there is also a physical threat. As we will get into in this chapter, Islam is a religion that rose to prominence through what I will term "conversion by conquest." It was through the militaristic conquest of people groups that Islam grew and became what it is today. In short, Islam is a religion where violence and martyrdom are incentivized, particularly violence toward anyone the Muslim sees as a threat to their religion, including Christians. However, before we get into that, it's important to start with the origins.

FOUNDATION OF ISLAM

The Islamic religion originated in a place known as the Arabian Peninsula, which is now present-day Yemen, Oman, Qatar, Bahrain, Kuwait, Saudi Arabia, the United Arab Emirates, and parts of Jordan and Iraq. Originally, this area was occupied by nomadic people groups who traveled to survive the climate. Around 5 BC, settlements began being established, and many chose Mecca because of its location near the west coast of Saudi Arabia. Essential to the establishment of Mecca was the creation of the Kaaba, which was a large shrine dedicated to the many spiritual deities the people worshiped. At this point in time, animistic polytheism was the prevailing religious belief system. In short, animism is the belief that all objects, places, animals, etc. have souls, and polytheism is the belief in many gods. Because of the location and religious significance of Mecca due to the Kaaba, Mecca became the religious center for the region. This began a pattern of people making pilgrimages to Mecca, which still proves significant for Muslims today.

Another defining fact of significance for Mecca is that Islam's founder, Muhammad, was born there. Muhammad was born in 570 AD to a widowed mother who died when he was six. He was subsequently raised by an uncle and lived with him throughout his adolescence. When Muhammad was twenty-five, he began working for a wealthy widow named Khadijah, whom he later married.

Once in his thirties, Muhammad began frequently going to the mountains outside of Mecca to meditate. On one particular trip at the age of forty, he came back from Mount Hira and said that he had been visited by the angel Gabriel. He stated that Gabriel commanded him to go proclaim the message of Islam. In short, this message was for people to turn from their paganism and polytheism, repent from evil, and worship Allah, whom Muhammad declared to be the one true god. Not surprisingly, this message was met with heavy resistance. He was instructing people to leave everything they held sacred and believed to be true and instructing them to believe a new set of religious ideas that was in direct contrast to what they held to be true.

The resistance became so bad that Muhammad fled to Medina to escape persecution. On the way to Medina, he encountered a fair amount of disadvantaged and hopeless people who were receptive to the message of Islam. They converted, and Muhammad trained them as they continued to Medina. When Muhammad arrived in Medina, he already had a sizeable group of Islamic adherents and was ready for the anticipated persecution he might receive.

Initially, the people of Medina met him with resistance, but Muhammad and his army defeated them. Once the tension and violence subsided, the residents of Medina realized that he was a good man and a capable leader, and they offered him citizenship. He refused, telling them he was only there for a short time. After his stint in Medina, he returned to Mecca with his army, conquered the city, and forced the people to convert. If they resisted or refused, he killed them and looted their property. Once Mecca was conquered, Muhammad continued this pattern of conquering territories and forcing people to convert. By the time he died in 632, he had conquered nearly the entire Arabian Peninsula. Within the next hundred years following his death, Muhammad's caliphs, or successors, had taken Islam from the Atlantic to the borders of China.

SPIRITUAL HISTORY

With the geographic history and foundational origins in mind, let's look now at the spiritual history. As I mentioned earlier, one of the intents of this chapter is to inform the reader regarding Islam by highlighting the differences that exist between Islam and Christianity. From a foundational standpoint, Islam and Christianity share some similarities until the Ishmael/Isaac split in the line of Abraham. In Genesis 15, God promises a child to Abraham (formerly Abram prior to his name change in Genesis 17) through his wife Sarah, who was barren at the time. In order for this child to be born, Sarah gave Abraham her maidservant Hagar, and Hagar conceived Ishmael (Gen. 16). Technically, God had given Abraham a child, but since the child did not come from Sarah, this was not the child of the covenant promise. In time, God gave Sarah a child named Isaac and thereby fulfilled His covenant promise with Abraham. Isaac was the child of promise. Isaac then eventually fathered Jacob, who was the father of the Twelve Tribes of Israel. Jesus Christ came into the world through the lineage of the Twelve Tribes, thus ultimately fulfilling the covenant between God and Abraham.

In Islam, the point of contention comes with who the child of promise was. Muslims believe that Ishmael was the child of promise. Muhammad came into the world through the line of Ishmael. So they believe that Muhammad is part of Allah's covenant promise.

This is a significant point of contention and has far-reaching implications in terms of differences in religious beliefs. For starters, the figureheads for each religion had vastly different ways of interacting with the people they were seeking to convert. Jesus preached a message of grace, love, and fellowship with God through repentance of sins. Jesus's primary tools of conversion involved His words and His actions, specifically the miracles He performed through casting out demons, feeding the masses, and raising the dead to life. Muhammad's primary method of conversion, as earlier stated, was military force. He did not perform miracles and did not preach a message of love and grace.

FIVE PILLARS

Let's look now at the qualifications for being a Muslim. A good starting point is the Five Pillars. These are the five things one must do in order to be considered a true Muslim. The first is known as Shahada, or the Declaration of Faith. This states that there is no god but Allah, and Muhammad is his messenger. The second is Salat, or prayer. Devout, true Muslims stop and pray five times a day: sunrise, noon, afternoon, sunset, and night. When praying, the individual is to face Mecca, specifically the Kaaba, and often does so in a bowed position. These prayers are much more structured and ritualistic than how Christians often think of praying. The third pillar is Zakat, or charity. This pillar instructs the Muslim to give to the poor and help improve the circumstances of the less fortunate. The fourth is Sawm, or fasting, most notably observed during the month of Ramadan, in which Muslims abstain from food and drink from sunrise to sunset. During this time, most will end the day by breaking the fast with other Muslims at a meal known as "Iftar." The fifth and final pillar, which makes sense in light of the history, is Hajj, or the Muslim's pilgrimage to Mecca. This pilgrimage is intended to be a sign of unity among Muslims and is a journey that all adult Muslims must take at least once if they are physically able and can afford to do so.

ARTICLES OF FAITH

Another central area of importance is the Articles of Faith. These are the six most important doctrines to which Muslims adhere. If it helps, think of them as a mission statement, so to speak. The first of these articles is God, or Tauheed. This deals with the belief in God and, more specifically, that there is one god, Allah. Within this is also the belief that Allah is so big that man is incapable of grasping any part of who he is, and he, therefore, is unknowable.

This is important because it points to a very foundational difference in Christianity and Islam, and that is man's ability to have relationship with God. This is one reason that the Christian message is often appealing to Muslims. Rather than a militant observer concerned with what people can do for him (Allah), Christianity presents a God who is utterly concerned with what He can do for His people. He knows that our only chance of redemption, righteousness, salvation, and the ability to truly do good in this life comes through relationship with Him, not through our independent efforts. Fortunately for the believer in Christ, He not only welcomes us in relationship but pursues us to accomplish this.

The second Article of Faith is the declaration of the existence of angels. This article states that angels are nonphysical beings. Many believe there are angels assigned to people to record one's good and bad deeds.

The third Article of Faith deals with the prophets. There are twenty-five in the Quran. It is not for the Muslim to distinguish between degree, but Muhammad is, without question, considered the greatest and last prophet.

The fourth is the belief in the Books. This is the belief that the holy scriptures of Islam have been inspired directly by God and dictated by the prophets. The scriptures include the writings of the Quran and the Hadith.

The fifth Article of Faith is the concept of a Judgment Day. For the Muslim, this means that Allah will hold everyone accountable for their bad deeds. There is a concept of mercy within this, and this is that Allah will omit certain bad deeds and multiply good deeds. However, the soteriology, or doctrine of salvation, is definitely works-based.

The final Article of Faith is Allah's decree. This states that Allah is sovereign and decides people's eternal fates. While Christianity asserts God's sovereignty, within this is also the mystery that humans have the freedom to choose to follow Christ.

The Five Pillars and the Articles of Faith are, in effect, the "by-laws" of Islam. They state the qualifications of the faith and the obligations of the adherent. Similar to the Ten Commandments and the Great Commission found in the Bible, the Five Pillars and Articles of Faith are concise ways of stating what is most important for the Muslim. Without sacred texts to support these claims, the claims would be meaningless. So let's look at these holy scriptures, where they came from, and what they mean for the Muslim.

QURAN

The most important text in the Islamic religion is the Quran. According to Islamic tradition, the Quran is the only text divinely inspired by Allah himself and was given to the prophet Muhammad through the Archangel Gabriel. Because of its line of direct transmission, Muslims believe that every word of the Quran is without error and, therefore, should not be translated lest a mistake be made. Nabeel Qureshi, in his book *Seeking Allah, Finding Jesus*, states the following regarding the Quran:

> Muslims believe that every single word of the Quran was
> dictated verbatim by Allah, through the Archangel Gabriel, to
> Muhammad. The Quran is therefore not only inspired at the
> level of meaning but at the deeper level of the words themselves.
> For this reason, Muslims do not consider the Quran translat-
> able. If it is rendered in any language other than Arabic, it is not
> Quran but rather an interpretation of the Quran. A book can be
> a true Quran only if written in Arabic (36).

So clearly, the Quran is extremely important and central to the Islamic faith. Many Muslims begin learning to recite the Quran at a very early age and are taught its significance in regards to Islam. Interesting to note, however, is that interpretation and questioning of the scriptures is not something that is encouraged for the majority of Muslims. It is reserved, rather, for the scholars. This points to a theme that you may begin to notice within the Islamic faith, and that is a lack of freedom. Christians, even though we believe in the concrete, foundational truth of Christ, are still given the freedom and even encouraged to question things to see if they are right, true, and from God. First John 4:1 states, "Beloved, do not believe every spirit, but test the spirits, whether they are of God; because many false prophets have gone out into the world." Islam does not encourage this type of thought, which also points to the militaristic rigor of the religion. Consider Qureshi's commentary on the topic:

> People from Eastern Islamic cultures generally assess truth through lines of authority, not individual reasoning… Leaders have done the critical reasoning, and leaders know best. Receiving input from multiple sources and then critically examining the data to distill a truth is an exercise for specialists, not the common man" (79).

This leads to a widespread trust and lack of questioning of not just the teachings of Islam but the Quran itself. This often, somewhat ironically, results in a lack of comprehensive knowledge of the Quran because of certain undesirable teachings that get far less attention than the appealing ones.

Rarely in life do we have characteristics that we reserve for certain areas and exclude from others. For example, if somebody is characteristically lazy, then they normally will not be the type of person who runs marathons or is the last one to leave the office. Or for someone who is characteristically friendly, they won't normally be friendly to certain people and rude to others. The same can be said of the Muslim who is taught not to questions things of religion. If they are taught not to question things of the Quran and the Islamic faith, then they will usually be less inclined to question and seek truth elsewhere. In other words, they won't go looking for outside truth in the form of Christianity as a result of questioning their own faith.

This, however, tends to add to the intrigue of the gospel message. When they are presented with a biblical message that contradicts what they have believed as truth in Islam, a new realm of enticing possibilities becomes a potential reality. It strikes a chord within our human nature to think freely. Humans are created to inherently desire freedom, and that extends to how we think. People don't generally like being told what to do and how to think, but if it is repeated enough and confirmed by experience and observation, we tend to just accept it as truth. When met with an appealing and alternate message, the desire to think freely is triggered, and the results can be positive.

HADITH

The other widely recognized sacred texts of Islam are the Hadith. The Hadith are texts that give accounts of the life of Muhammad. They are similar to the Bible in that they are considered to be divinely inspired but written by men, whereas the Quran is said to be the direct words of Allah dictated verbatim by Muhammad. The Hadith contain the traditions of Islam. This ranges from marital restrictions to civil lawsuits to apostasy and the ways in which to handle such situations.

Because of the content in the Hadith and the number considered authentic (approximately one thousand to a little more than four thousand depending on the school of thought), the origin of different sects of Islam can often be traced back to differences in interpretation of the various Hadith. Much of the discrepancy regarding interpretation deals with deciding which Hadith are authentic and which are not. This is done through analyzing the chain of transmission, or in other words, how it was recorded, how it was passed down, and whether it is trustworthy. This process is known as isnad. You can probably imagine how this might cause division. If these texts largely define how one lives and interacts with the world as a Muslim, discrediting a Hadith because of one's personal discernment of its legitimacy can be a touchy subject. I say this to highlight the importance that these texts have for the Muslim. Regardless of the ones to which the Muslim adheres, the Hadith are highly valued and lead the Muslim in the way he or she should live by giving direct account of Muhammad's life.

SHARIA LAW

Now, we'll look at some of the more controversial ideology within Islam. Often, the negative associations that come with Islam deal with Sharia law and jihad. We'll begin with Sharia law.

Sharia law, in short, defines how a Muslim should live his or her life. The instructions on how to live can range anywhere from a woman having to wear a hijab to cover her head or parts of her face to the duty of a family or community to kill a fellow Muslim for apostasy (leaving the faith). One thing that makes Sharia law interesting, and why I won't get into the specifics of what this looks like for the Muslim on an individual level, is that there is no single written document of Sharia law. That is not to say that certain groups have not defined and written down their own versions, but there is no one single unifying document that details Sharia law for every Muslim. For Christians, the closest single, independently-standing set of instructions that we have is the Ten Commandments. All Christians are to abide by the Ten Commandments, not just certain Christians. Sharia law doesn't quite work that way.

There are some things within the broad spectrum of Sharia law that are universal. For example, all four major Sunni schools of thought and all three major Shia ones believe that an individual should be killed for apostasy. The reason that other issues aren't agreed upon across the board goes back to the interpretation of the holy texts. Sharia law is derived first from the Quran, then from the Hadith, and then the ulema, or the Muslim scholars. Different interpretations of the texts lead to different beliefs in Sharia law. Regardless of a particular sect's interpretation, Sharia law is something that each Muslim school of thought takes very seriously.

JIHAD

Next is the concept of jihad. Jihad tends to get a lot of attention due to its association with violence. The controversy over whether Islam is a religion of peace or violence is born out of opinions regarding the concept of jihad.

The word "jihad" means to struggle or strive, particularly for the sake of Allah. The peaceful connotations of the word deal with the service-oriented aspects of the faith. This could be anything from maintaining the mosque one attends (9:19) to taking care of widows. However, if you look at chapter 9 of the Quran, verse 19 makes it clear which is more important. The verse states, "Do you consider giving water to pilgrims and maintaining the Sacred Mosque the same as believing in God and the Last Day and striving in God's path? They are not equal in God's sight. God does not guide the unjust people." While this is not saying that caring for people in need and keeping up the mosque are bad things, it is saying that they are not as important as doing whatever is necessary to strive in God's path.

When dealing with this concept of striving for Allah, the highest form of service centers around violence. Often in the Quran, the call to jihad is a call to physically fight anything threatening the belief system of Islam. In addition to this, one of the most highly regarded and trustworthy Hadith compilations, Sahih Bukhari, makes clear the significance of a Muslim's engagement in violence for the sake of Allah. Remember that while not considered as important as the Quran, the Hadith serve as a highly-valued complement to the Quran, and according to many Muslims, even necessary to live the Islamic life. In volume 4, book 52 of Sahih Bukhari, we see the Muslim's incentive for violence. The glorification of martyrdom is a significant theme throughout. Consider the following:

Narrated by Samura

The Prophet said, "Last night two men came to me (in a dream) and made me ascend a tree and then admitted me into a better and superior house, better of which I have never seen. One of them said, 'This house is the house of martyrs.'" (49)

Narrated by Anas bin Malik

The Prophet said, "A single endeavor (of fighting) in Allah's Cause in the forenoon or in the afternoon is better than the world and whatever is in it." (50)

Narrated by Anas bin Malik

The Prophet said, "Nobody who dies and finds good from Allah (in the Hereafter) would wish to come back to this world even if he were given the whole world and whatever is in it, except the martyr who, on seeing the superiority of martyrdom, would like to come back to the world and get killed again (in Allah's Cause)." Narrated Anas: The Prophet said, "A single endeavor (of fighting) in Allah's Cause in the afternoon or in the forenoon is better than all the world and whatever is in it. A place in Paradise as small as the bow or lash of one of you is better than all the world and whatever is in it. And if a houri from Paradise appeared to the people of the earth, she would fill the space between Heaven and the Earth with light and pleasant scent and her head cover is better than the world and whatever is in it." (53)

Narrated by Abu Huraira

The Prophet said, "By Him in Whose Hands my life is! Were it not for some men amongst the believers who dislike to be left behind me and whom I cannot provide with means of conveyance, I would certainly never remain behind any Sariya' (army-unit) setting out in Allah's Cause. By Him in Whose Hands my life is! I would love to be martyred in Allah's Cause and then get resurrected and then get martyred, and then get resurrected again and then get martyred and then get resurrected again and then get martyred." (54)

In these passages there is a clear emphasis on the afterlife. In both Christianity and Islam, as well as most major world religions including Buddhism and Hinduism, there is at least some concept of an afterlife. It's most concrete in Christianity, meaning that those who do not believe that Christ is the Son of God and obey His teachings accordingly will be eternally separated from God in hell, and those that do believe and obey will spend eternity in His presence in heaven. In Islam there is a heaven and hell, but entry is based upon merit, or Allah's judgment of one's good deeds versus their bad. Add to this the fact that on Judgment Day Allah may multiply certain good deeds and lessen certain bad ones, and it gets less clearly defined who gains entrance and who does not. Hinduism and Buddhism, in short, both ascribe to the belief that one reaches nirvana, a state without suffering, through a process of reincarnation. Regardless of the religious beliefs to which one ascribes, the intent is to reach a place free from suffering. Just as escaping the suffering-ridden world in which we live is a powerful motivator for many to adhere to religious beliefs, so too is the idea of a present, ongoing eternity either marked by suffering or joy.

In the context of these Sahih Bukhari passages, jihad is tied to martyrdom, and martyrdom is glorified. Even further, jihad, in the context of martyrdom, is incentivized. Not only does it immediately gain the martyr entrance into paradise, it grants him or her immediate access into the best that eternal paradise has to offer. To be clear, in these passages, this promise is geared more toward the martyr who dies in battle rather than in persecution. Anyone who claims Islam is a religion of peace simply has either not studied the life of Muhammad and his teachings or has chosen to ignore or take them out of context. The ideology surrounding the teachings of jihad is the same mentality that fueled the hand grenade incident at the crusade.

ISLAM VS. CHRISTIANITY

With a solid foundation for the history and beliefs of Islam established, let's look at some of the core components of Islam and Christianity, how they align with how we operate as individuals, and how they compare with each other as a result. My intent is to highlight the weaknesses of Islam and also point out the ways in which Christianity not only addresses those weaknesses but triumphs over them. To accomplish this, I will first define the purposes of religion and then look at the messages of both religious figureheads, the soteriology of each, and the role that love plays in establishing the legitimacy of a religion.

While there are many purposes of religion, the two main ones that I will focus on are identity and salvation. Religion, or the absence of, provides identity. As we discussed earlier, humans are drawn to the pursuit of identity. We seek to find ways to associate ourselves with others through material possessions, communal interests, and religious beliefs. Religion automatically takes care of two of these three. Obviously, it attaches one to religious beliefs, but it also makes someone part of a community. Even for an atheist or agnostic, there are the beliefs against the existence of a specific higher power and organized religion, as well as an automatic association with like-minded people.

The case for Islam's appeal from an identity standpoint is very strong. In many ways, I would argue that it is stronger than Christianity's. One reason for this is the amount of tradition Islam contains. For devout Muslims, this tends to lead to a strong sense of unity. I say devout because it does not really apply to someone who doesn't take the practices seriously. If taken seriously, however, things such as the five daily prayers and the month of Ramadan provide significant community and identity. They bring people together and provide tangible elements of group identity.

Christianity does not really have this to the same extent that Islam does.

Christianity certainly gives one identity with a group of like-minded people, but there are not as many outward, public, corporate expressions of Christianity. Regardless, both religions share the characteristic of drawing people in through the promise of identity.

Religion also provides one with some type of salvation. The English Oxford Dictionary defines salvation as "preservation or deliverance from harm, ruin, or loss" (en.oxforddictionaries.com). This is true for both the Muslim and Christian, as salvation means an eternity spent in each religion's respective heaven. It is true for the Buddhist and the Hindu, in the sense that harm comes from the pursuit of personal desire and pleasure. The salvation would be freeing oneself from this harm by ridding oneself of desire and, thus, being saved from it. In atheism, there is the belief that there is harm in adhering to organized religion. The salvation, so to speak, in atheism lies within the idea that one is freed from the harm of organized religion by believing in the existence of nothing. For any religion, the draw of salvation from a conceptual standpoint is strong largely due to the security and finality that it provides. It takes the individual from a place of not knowing to a place of security.

So the overarching case for religion has been set: people desire identity and salvation. Islam and Christianity both provide this is in the clearest, most tangible sense. Let's now look at why I believe Christianity to be superior to Islam and, thus, the only true religious belief system acknowledging the one and only true God. This section may get a bit academic at times, but I will do my best to explain everything as clearly as possible.

We will first look at the similarities between the prophets. Muhammad and Jesus Christ are, respectively, the most important human figures in Islam and Christianity. Both Muhammad and Jesus are said to have existed on this earth in human form. This means that they walked, talked, breathed, ate, etc. as you and I do today. Both also claimed to possess divine revelation. For Jesus, this means that He is said to have been the direct mouthpiece of God and spoke God's words exactly as God gave them to Him. The same is said of Muhammad's role in communicating the words of Allah. This was something of which other humans were not capable.

Also, as the figureheads of their respective religions, both serve as the ultimate model for how to live one's life. Both are said to come from the line of Abraham, and both spent their lives on earth in what is considered today as the Middle East.

In addition to their similarities as individuals, there are also similarities in their teachings. Both advocate for being kind and doing good. Both teach that believing in and adhering to their respective messages is a necessary part of salvation. Both also teach monotheism, or that there is only one God. They also share some beliefs on eternity, namely that eternity is better than the present and that heaven and hell are real.

The differences in their teachings, however, are significant and have profound implications. One of the most significant deals with their teachings on how God relates to people. Islam portrays Allah as distant and not interested in relationship with mankind. A large part of this stems from their theology regarding Allah's holiness. According to Islamic theology, it would be an insult to think that Allah would stoop down to the level of man and engage him/her in relationship because this would be below him.

Christians, on the other hand, while still believing in God's sovereignty and holiness, believe that His desire to have relationship with His people is a central part of who He is. Rather than view it as "lesser" that He would stoop down from heaven to pursue relationship with us, we see it as a testament to His character: that He is good, loving, and compassionate. Christians believe that God desires relationship with us so much that He came to the earth in the human form of His Son Jesus Christ and died to make relationship with Him available. This is an invitation open to all who would repent and believe upon Him for their salvation. This is, in large part, why Christianity can be so offensive to Muslims. In their eyes, it is blasphemy to suggest that God would leave heaven to make Himself available to us. For Christians, it is the foundation of the assurance we have that God is for us and not against us.

SOTERIOLOGY

Soteriology is a fancy word for the doctrine of salvation, which is a fancy way of saying the way(s) in which we are saved. Another way of thinking about salvation is that it is how we move from a place of not being accepted by God to a place of acceptance. To reiterate, in Christianity salvation is attained through repentance of sins and faith in the life, death, and resurrection of Jesus Christ. In Islam, salvation is attained by outweighing bad deeds with good ones. This is how the Muslim pleases Allah. In theory, this is done by strictly adhering to the Five Pillars and the Articles of Faith, with martyrdom being the ultimate way that one gains favor and, thereby, salvation from Allah.

LOVE IS A POWERFUL MOTIVATOR

The ultimate difference between Islam and Christianity comes down to love. This is what separates Christianity from every other religion and why Christianity proves triumphant over Islam and all other religious systems. People are created with a desire to be loved. Every person on this earth, whether Muslim, Christian, atheist, or other, has a desire to be loved. This is why we seek out relationships. This is why it hurts when someone we care about disappoints us. We are designed to desire and be affected by love.

A central aspect of Christian creationism is that man was and still is created in the image of God. If man is created in the image of God and has an inherent desire to give and receive love, then that must mean that love is also a part of God's character. Most Muslims do not believe that Allah created man fully in his image because there are some qualities that man is impossible of possessing due to Allah's supremacy. This means that theoretically man could have the desire to be loved even if Allah is not truly loving. However, the Christian argument is that if one of our positive attributes as people is the capacity for love, then the God that we serve must be loving because we are created in His image. This tends to be a compelling message for someone who has never thought of God as someone who loves them but rather as one whom they serve out of duty. Because we have been made to love and be loved, we will always be affected by true, deep, genuine love. It has the power to break down the strongest walls and soften the hardest of hearts.

Think for a moment about some of the things in your life that you love the most. Perhaps your family and friends come to mind. Maybe you love your pets or the city in which you live. Regardless, whatever you love likely draws things out of you that ordinary things in your life do not. For example, if one of your best friends has a flat tire in the middle of the night, you will likely sacrifice sleep to help them. Or you may be willing to work at a job that you do not like so that you can provide for your family. These are just examples, and each person is motivated by different things, but regardless, when we love something, we will often go to great links to ensure that the relationship with our object of affection stays in good graces. When true love exists, people both act and are affected in ways that surpass normal interaction with people and things in this world.

Islam is a religion void of love. The concept of true love does not exist. The concepts of Allah being omnipresent (everywhere), omnipotent (all-powerful), and omniscient (all-knowing) exist, but the concept of a deep love between Allah and his people does not. This is why the Christian message can be so powerful to Muslims. Not only do we proclaim that our God, the one true God, contains all of the characteristics and power of their god but also that the God of Christianity loves and deeply desires relationship with His people. Furthermore, He loves them so much that He stepped down from heaven in the form of His Son Jesus Christ and died for them so that this relationship would be available. The work of the Holy Spirit in one's life and the message of love and relationship with God are undeniably appealing to the Muslim who walks through life wondering if what they are doing is enough to please the one that they dedicate their life to serve. To be clear, this message is true not just for Muslims but for all mankind. All who repent of their sins and confess Jesus Christ as Lord and Savior of their life are immediately ushered into relationship with God. It is not about what we can do for God (although our obedience and service to Him are important) but what God has done for us through Christ. In villages where the power of Islamic deception has ruled for generations, I have seen the power of Christ come and break even the greatest of strongholds. While He uses believers around the world and even me to accomplish His purposes, it is the power of the Holy Spirit that comes and makes these great miracles a reality.

LOVE IS A GIFT

While the message of the love found in relationship with Christ is certainly appealing, if we did not model this in our lives, it likely would not connect. As the saying goes, "Actions speak louder than words." Making true, radical love a central part of our lives and ministry often opens the door for relationships and chances to share the gospel. We aim to love people in such a way that they are stimulated to ask questions.

One of the main ways we do this is through using our resources to give gifts to those in the community. These gifts are items that are highly beneficial to their daily lives but are often difficult for them to acquire on their own. One of our primary gifts is mosquito netting. Mosquitos are a problem in our community. For people with no measures of protection, this can make it difficult to sleep at night and make them more susceptible to mosquito-borne illnesses such as malaria. While mosquito nets seem like an easy purchase, many have to focus so much on the primary necessities (food, water, shelter, clothing) that they cannot afford to purchase mosquito nets.

Perhaps the main reason the giving of gifts is so effective is because it doesn't make sense to someone outside of Christianity, particularly a Muslim. The gifts are completely unmerited. When they receive these gifts, one of the first questions they often ask, even if not verbalized, is, "Why?" They recognize that they have not done anything to earn these gifts, so it does not make sense. When we tell them we do what we do because of Christ's love for us and for them, it only adds to the intrigue. People outside the Christian faith, particularly Muslims, are not taught to love Christians. Christians, on the other hand, are taught to love all people. In fact, we are even instructed to love those who don't love us. Luke 6:32 states, "But if you love those who love you, what credit is that to you? For even sinners love those who love them."

The dynamic of love through the giving of gifts sometimes does open the door to the salvation of those receiving the gifts. When this happens, this is surely a time of celebration. Often times, if it does not directly lead to the salvation of the recipients, it opens the door for us to be well received by the communities that we serve. This leads to the communities trusting us, which leads to relationships. These relationships lead to continued ministry, which often leads to the salvation of those to whom we minister.

In addition to mosquito nets, we also give out mattresses, school supplies and uniforms, and pay for school fees. It does not always happen overnight, but this opens the door for further relationships. It is our desire to get to know the people who receive the gifts. Many of the children whose school fees we pay for are orphans or have extremely broken family situations. Paying the fees and providing the children with the necessary supplies to attend school opens the door for us to enter their lives and the lives of those who care for them. It is in these times that we are able to not only display the love of Christ through relationship but also explain the gospel, answer any questions they have, and pray with them.

One time early in our ministry, we entered a village equipped with mattresses to give to those in need. We gave them to the children of the village, and they carried them to their homes. This caused quite a stir in the community. People came out of their homes to see who had provided the mattresses. They were surprised to learn that they had come not from one of the local mosques but from the local Christians. This initial shock quickly turned to intrigue, which turned into the villagers seeing us as a source of help rather than the mosques. Once this happened, the villagers were willing and even eager to hear the life-saving gospel of Jesus Christ.

SECTION THREE

references

chapter twelve:
introduction to references

As you know, one of the major intents of this book is to encourage the reader to consider his or her worldview. Since all those involved with the creation of the book see the world from a Christian perspective, it is important to include an overview of the foundation of these beliefs. This chapter will provide a summary of some of the major themes of the Bible that are necessary to understanding Christianity. I will attempt to answer basic questions about Christian theology that may have arisen during the reading of the book. The rest of the "References" section will contain vital information on the unseen spiritual realm as well as the Christian's role therein. For many readers, this will likely be new information (or at least more in-depth), and I pray that you will read, study, meditate, and pray over the information as you receive it. Ultimately, we hope that this portion of the book will direct you to the Bible and encourage you to experience the life-giving power of God's Word. Scripture references will be given for each section at the end of the chapter.

CREATION

"In the beginning God created the heavens and the earth" (Gen. 1:1). These are the opening words of the Bible found in Genesis 1. Right from the start the Bible establishes that it is God who is the Creator and, thus, controller of this world. He spoke the world and everything in it into being, from the mountains and seas to the people and animals inhabiting it. He created Adam as the first representative of mankind and gave him dominion over "every living thing that moves on the earth" (Gen. 1:28). God then decided that it was not suitable for man to be alone and created woman as a helper for him (Gen. 2:18). Out of Adam, God made Eve, and they lived in perfect harmony with each other and with God in the garden of Eden (Gen. 2:22).

––––––––––

It is important to note that from the beginning God the Father, God the Son, and God the Holy Spirit existed with each other in perfect harmony. These three (Trinity) form the Godhead. Each are equal in power and the same in nature. They are eternally loving, just, and pure, without any fault, blemish, or sin. Each has specific roles that combine to accomplish the specific purposes laid out by God before the foundations of the earth. God the Father is the overseer, the creator, and the originator of the heavens and the earth (Gen. 1:1). Jesus Christ, the Son of God, was sent by God the Father to die a cruel death on the cross to provide salvation and eternal life for all who believe in Him (John 3:16). The Holy Spirit has several roles. When a person receives Christ, the Holy Spirit comes to dwell in that person and works in them to make them more like Christ (Rom. 8:11). The Spirit also convicts the believer of sin (John 16:7–11), enables the believer to live a holy life (Rom. 15:16), cultivates the fruits of the Spirit (Gal. 5:16–24), and helps the believer to pray (Rom. 8:26).

––––––––––

At the beginning of creation, God and man existed in perfect harmony because there was no sin. Before the fall of Adam and Eve into sin, there was no enmity or separation between God and man, nor were there any by-products of sin such as death, sickness, conflict, and pride.

THE FALL OF SATAN

Before getting into the actual fall of Adam and Eve into sin, it is important to detail the origin of Satan. Satan was a being created by God and originally a good angel who went by the name Lucifer. In God's original heavenly design, there were three archangels. These archangels were given special responsibility and authority over other angels. Lucifer was one of these archangels. Within the hierarchy of archangels, Lucifer was the highest followed by Michael and then Gabriel. Lucifer was a Cherubim, or covering/protecting angel, who stood before God ministering to Him with worship.

Eventually, pride arose from within him, and he became envious of God's power, majesty, and authority over the heavenly realms. He desired to be worshiped as God was, and this pride caused him to believe that he could overcome his Creator. As one of three archangels, Lucifer had access to one-third of the angels of which he was in charge. He used this access and power to convince these angels to join him in his rebellion. He told them he would "ascend into heaven" and "exalt [his] throne above the stars of God" (Isaiah 14:13). He goes on in verse 14 to say that he will "be like the Most High." In other words, he convinced the angels under his control that he would become God.

So he and one-third of the angels rebelled. God quickly subdued the rebellion and cast Lucifer and the angels with him out of heaven. After being thrown out of heaven, his name was changed from Lucifer, which means "morning star," to Satan, which means "adversary." Banned from heaven and unable to overcome God, Satan decided that attacking mankind would be the easiest way to frustrate God; thus, enter Adam and Eve.

THE FALL OF MAN

Before the fall, God told Adam and Eve that they could eat from any tree in the garden except for the tree of the knowledge of good and evil (Gen. 2:16–17). One day as Adam and Eve were walking in the garden, Satan, embodying a snake, came to them and began to call into question what God had told them (Genesis 3:1–5). He twisted God's words, and in a moment of weakness, they succumbed to Satan's temptation and ate from the tree of forbidden fruit (Gen. 3:6). This immediately granted Satan access to God's created people. Prior to this act God enjoyed perfect communion with Adam and Eve because of their purity. They were without blemish, and God dwelled in their presence and they in His.

When sin came into the world through Adam and Eve, the condition of the world was forever changed. To put it into perspective, consider this example. Let's look at the life of someone who struggles with addiction to alcohol. In this person's life, there was surely a span of time where he or she had no exposure to alcohol, and therefore did not experience a desire to drink. They lived life free from its grip and the damage that addiction brings, and their life was better for it.

However, when they reached the age of having their first drink, an entirely new world of addiction and the consequences that come with it began to be experienced. This first exposure is all it takes for the door to be opened to all the damage, pain, and shame that addiction often brings. In effect, the same was true with Adam and Eve. Prior to the eating of the forbidden fruit, they only knew purity and love. They only knew relationships without conflict, jealousy, or insecurity. However, when Eve ate the fruit of the tree of the knowledge of good and evil, an entirely new world of sin and the consequences that came with it were revealed.

Another way to put it is that God gave His people dominion over the earth so that they could bring His kingdom to reality on the earth. Unfortunately, when Adam and Eve chose sin, they were choosing to follow Satan in his rebellion. By doing this, they surrendered their God-given dominion to Satan.

There is somewhat of a rabbit trail of implications that comes with this. As I said earlier, when sin entered the world so did death and separation from God. What this means is that if mankind was separated from God at the point when sin entered the world, then each person born from that point forward entered the world separated from God and unable to please Him on his or her own. Because of our sin nature inherited from Adam and Eve, we are not born into this world seeking God or the things of God. If we are not born seeking the kingdom of God, then we must be born seeking the kingdom of darkness. We are born with an inclination to disobey God and, in the process, harm ourselves and others, even if we are unaware of it at the time. We are inclined to pride, selfishness, lust, envy, insecurity, anger, and so on. This eventually leads to death, and no man can prevent death or its consequences. Thus, enter Jesus Christ.

THE SIGNIFICANCE OF CHRIST

Although we are born into sin and separated from God, in His loving-kindness He provided a way for regained access to Him. This was through the death and resurrection of His Son, Jesus Christ. In order for sin to be atoned, or paid for, a sacrifice had to take place. Romans 6:23 states, "For the wages of sin is death, but the gift of God is eternal life in Christ Jesus our Lord." If the wages, or payment, of sin is death, then it would stand to reason that the only just payment for the cleansing of sin would be the death of one without sin.

Sinning against God is the highest form of offense that one can commit. If God is the Creator and giver of human life, and He is, then this makes Him the ultimate authority in both the spiritual and physical world. Committing an offense against the highest authority automatically increases the severity of the offense, regardless of the action. Although this does not always manifest itself in modern societies, divine and natural law both support the belief that the greater the severity of the offense, the greater the severity of the consequence. This is why people don't receive life sentences in prison for breaking into someone's car. It wasn't as if Adam and Eve solely brought sickness or violence into the world. Their sin brought every ill thing one can think of into the world: sickness, violence, pride, divorce, war, and the most significant of all, death and separation from God. This is why God, in His love, sent His only Son to be beaten, humiliated, and ultimately die a torturous death on a cross. This was the only way to atone for sin. If the sacrifice for sin was inconsiderable, then it would seemingly compromise or call into question God's attitude toward sin. Furthermore, it would also be less likely to convict and penetrate the heart of an individual if the sacrifice was insignificant. Jesus addressed this in Luke 7:41–43 when He told the story of a moneylender who had two debtors.

The story goes like this:

> "There was a certain creditor who had two debtors. One owed five hundred denarii, and the other fifty. And when they had nothing with which to repay, he freely forgave them both. Tell Me, therefore, which of them will love him more?"
>
> Simon answered and said, "I suppose the one whom he forgave more."
>
> And He said to him, "You have rightly judged."

In the condition of each man or woman as a sinner, when one realizes the magnitude of Christ's sacrifice, he or she is then led to a deeper realization of just how much he or she has been forgiven. This, in turn, leads to a deeper understanding and appreciation of the grace we have been shown and, thus, leads to a deeper faith and desire to obey God.

In addition to Christ's death, equally important is His resurrection. Blood had to be shed for sins to be forgiven, and resurrection had to occur for death to be defeated (1 Cor. 15:20–22). As I said earlier, no man can prevent death or its consequences. God demonstrated His power and authority over something that is both inevitable and out of man's control by raising Christ from the dead. It was a

91

tangible demonstration that God has the final say in not only what occurs in life but also in death. It was also a taste of what is to come in the future for those who trust in Jesus Christ as their Lord and Savior, which is the redemption of all things broken (Col. 1:20).

Lastly, Christ's sacrifice on the cross provides a way for regained access to relationship with the Father. In John 14:6 Jesus says, "I am the way, the truth, and the life. No one comes to the Father except through Me." This verse makes clear that Christ is the only way to God. Furthermore, Romans 5:10–11 makes clear that not only is Christ the only way to God, but it was His death on the cross that accomplished this reconciliation. The verses state:

> For if when we were enemies we were reconciled to God
> through the death of His Son, much more, having been rec-
> onciled, we shall be saved by His life. And not only that, but
> we also rejoice in God through our Lord Jesus Christ, through
> whom we have now received the reconciliation.

When an individual chooses to believe upon Christ for his or her salvation, the Holy Spirit comes to indwell that person and, in the process, seals him or her in the Lord. The salvation process involves all three parts of the Trinity. The father draws the individual (John 6:44), Christ's death cleanses and saves (Rom. 5:10–11, 1 Peter 3:18), and the Holy Spirit seals, or ensures and keeps, the person in this salvation (2 Cor. 1:21–22).

GOD'S PLAN FOR REDEMPTION

In God's resurrection of Christ from the dead, He gave us a picture of His future redemption of the broken world in which we now live. In Revelation 21:1–4 John states,

> Now I saw a new heaven and a new earth, for the first heaven
> and the first earth had passed away. Also there was no more
> sea. Then I, John, saw the holy city, New Jerusalem, coming
> down out of heaven from God, prepared as a bride adorned
> for her husband. And I heard a loud voice from heaven saying,
> "Behold, the tabernacle of God is with men, and He will dwell
> with them, and they shall be His people. God Himself will be

with them and be their God. And God will wipe away every tear from their eyes; there shall be no more death, nor sorrow, nor crying. There shall be no more pain, for the former things have passed away.

This passage demonstrates that God is not only restoring the physical earth, hence the "holy city" coming down from heaven, but He is also restoring all the ills that plague mankind, including death, as seen in verse four. Verse five of the same chapter goes on to say that He "make[s] all things new" (Rev. 21:5). In other words, God's plans and purposes are to undo all the harm that came with the fall of man, restore things to how they were before sin entered the world, and dwell in perfect harmony with His people who believed upon Christ. He demonstrated that through the death of Christ and is still active in redeeming the world until the return of Christ.

chapter thirteen: satan

Satan's influence upon the world is real. Although he is already a foe defeated by the blood of Jesus Christ, he is still hard at work to keep people away from salvation in Christ. In order to effectively fight the powers of darkness, it is important to understand Satan, his origin, his methods, and his ultimate goal for the people of the earth. The more knowledgeable we are, the better equipped we are to fight. In an American football game, if the defense knew what play the offense would run before they ran it, it would be very hard for the offense to score. The same principle applies here. Before getting into this, let's briefly review what we've covered so far:

1. Lucifer and one-third of the angels under his control rebelled against God, were cast out of heaven, and Lucifer's name was changed to Satan, which means "adversary."

2. God's first created people, Adam and Eve, lived in perfect harmony with God in the Garden of Eden.

3. Satan tempted Adam and Eve into sin.

4. When Adam and Eve believed Satan's lies and ate from the tree of the knowledge of good and evil, sin and all its consequences entered the world.

5. When they did this, they surrendered their God-given dominion over the earth to Satan.

6. We are now born with a sinful nature and separated from God until salvation in Christ.

Adam and Eve's sin gave Satan dominion over the earth. Satan now "walks about like a roaring lion, seeking whom he may devour" and does this primarily by enticing us into sinful behavior (1 Peter 5:8). This is his main way of attempting to thwart God's plans for His people on earth.

Sin, in a big-picture sense, leads to two things: natural death and separation from God. When Adam and Eve sinned, death entered the world, and they were separated from the perfect fellowship they had with God. Sin also has consequences in the here-and-now, but the most significant of those consequences are the eternal ones. This is why Satan wants us to remain sinners. If an individual never recognizes his or her sin, never repents, and never comes to faith in Jesus Christ, then he or she will be separated from God in eternity. Satan knows this. His goal is always to steal, kill, and destroy, and he accomplishes this by keeping people in the bondage of sin.

Salvation in Christ removes Satan's curse of sin and death from over us. This means that God no longer sees us as sinners but as saints. This salvation begins with repentance. In order to repent of sin and come to faith in Christ, one has to first be aware that it exists. Awareness, however, is only the beginning of the battle. After becoming aware of our sin, it is vital to come to an understanding of how sin works. Understanding how sin works is crucial if we are to fight the constant temptations Satan and his demons throw our way.

HOW SIN WORKS

The first thing to note is that sin will always look appealing. In other words, sin is deceptive. Deception was the initial tactic Satan used against Adam and Eve, and it worked. The forbidden fruit looked appealing, but eating it brought death and destruction. Adam and Eve knew they had been told not to eat it, but Satan convinced them otherwise. His tactics are still the same today. He makes sin look appealing while hiding its true consequences. Think about the example of addiction from the opening chapter of this section. The object of addiction, regardless of what it is, always looks appealing and feels good in the moment. If it didn't, then it would have no power over people. In the end, however, the pursuit of sinful things brings brokenness and pain.

Proverbs 23:29–35 sums this idea up well. Consider these verses:

Who has woe?
Who has sorrow?

Who has contentions?
Who has complaints?
Who has wounds without cause?
Who has redness of eyes?
Those who linger long at the wine,
Those who go in search of mixed wine.
Do not look on the wine when it is red,
When it sparkles in the cup,
When it swirls around smoothly;
At the last it bites like a serpent,
And stings like a viper.
Your eyes will see strange things,
And your heart will utter perverse things.
Yes, you will be like one who lies down in the midst of the sea,
Or like one who lies at the top of the mast, saying:
"They have struck me, but I was not hurt;
They have beaten me, but I did not feel it.
When shall I awake, that I may seek another drink?

These verses discuss the woes that come with constant drunkenness. The section opens and closes with talking about the problems that come with drinking too much, which the Bible says is sinful. Notice in the middle of the passage, in verse 31, the instruction to "not look on the wine when it is red, when it sparkles in the cup... and swirls around smoothly." Why? Because it deceives us, and this deception leads to pain and brokenness.

The last line is also very important. The passage ends with the subject saying that he "may seek another drink." The pattern of sin that Satan draws people into not only leads to brokenness but also to a pattern of people trying to be their own savior. Notice that the drunkard does not end the passage by saying that he needs God; he ends the passage by saying that he needs another drink. He's become so entrapped by his sin that he returns to the sin as a way out.

The second thing to note is that Satan uses the origin of his original sin to his advantage over us. This origin is pride. When Satan was still Lucifer and was still in heaven, he became envious of God's position and thought he deserved to be on the same level as God. This is the essence of pride. We make ourselves great in our mind, desire things not intended for us, and become our own perceived savior.

The core message of the gospel is that we can't save ourselves and need someone greater to do this for us. This is why, out of His love and grace, God sent His Son Jesus Christ to die for us. When we sin, we are saying, whether we realize it or not, that we know what's best for us. We are declaring that we know best what will satisfy us and that our actions are what will accomplish this. We become discontent with God's position as God, which includes His principles for our lives, and we act disobediently in response.

Is this not what Satan did? He became discontent with God's position as God, acted out in disobedience, and suffered serious consequences. This is the same way Satan tempts us into sin today. He makes worldly things look appealing, draws us into considering them as viable options for our pleasure and satisfaction, convinces us that they will satisfy, and then we act in disobedience (sin) and suffer the consequences. This, to be clear, is the process that takes place when we sin. We have a choice not to believe Satan's lies. Let's look now, however, at the foot soldiers, so to speak, that Satan uses to attack and corrupt creation: his demons.

chapter fourteen:
demons

Satan is not alone in his attack against God's creation. He is joined by the angels who originally rebelled with him and were cast out of heaven. These fallen angels are known as demons. They comprise the army that makes up the Satanic kingdom. While Satan is the mastermind behind the evil that befalls the world, the demons are the ones that make it happen, so to speak.

Demons were originally created by God as eternal angelic beings. Like Lucifer, they existed in heaven with God until their rebellion. Although they have the same attributes as holy angels, they are fallen and evil and, thus, completely different in nature. While God's angels work for good, demons work for evil. Let's look now at some of these attributes and abilities.

The first thing worth noting is that demons themselves are invisible, but they can appear as animals, fearful creatures, other people, etc. They do this to accomplish their assigned purposes on earth. For example, they can appear as animals in the road and cause people to have wrecks. They can appear and disappear in this manner on an as-needed basis in order to accomplish their assigned tasks, which are ordered by Satan.

In terms of personal attributes, they do not eat, drink, or breathe. They are weightless and do not tire or age. This gives them the ability to constantly be on the move if ordered by Satan. They have all five human senses (seeing, hearing, feeling, smelling, tasting) but on a much higher level than humans. They also have the ability to speak. They use this to communicate with each other and to speak through human beings, who may not be aware that this demonic speech is taking place. The last attribute worth noting is that some have wings.

Now that we've looked at their personal characteristics, let's look at their structural attributes. By structural, I mean that there is organization in the Satanic hierarchy. Demons do not operate by happenstance. They are assigned specific tasks to carry out in specific geographic areas. If a demon fails to abide by these instructions, there are consequences.

By nature, demons are territorial. They structure their organization in accord with the human design. Humans organize by country, state, city, community, neighborhood, etc. Demons do the same. Since demons do not die, once they are assigned a location, they stay there eternally. If a strong, Spirit-filled church emerges in a particular area, then the demons in that area may be weakened. In that case, instead of leaving, the weakened demons may ask neighboring demons for help. They are very loyal to their area. Within the demonic hierarchy in these geographic locations, senior demons have lesser demons who move through neighborhoods seeking someone to attack. Their goal is to draw people in to the point where they can use humans as their foot soldiers. This is known as demonic possession.

POSSESSION

Aside from death, the most powerful method of demonic influence is possession. Possession is different from temptation, torment, and oppression. In these cases, the individual has not given him/herself over completely to demonic control. To possess something is to own it. So true demonic possession is when demons have entered a person and have ownership over that person. They influence and control the person's thoughts, actions, and behaviors. This is Satan's best attempt to thwart God's plan for His people because it not only affects the one possessed but also others in the path of the possessed.

This, however, is not an overnight happening. There is a process, and it starts with human choice. As with other manifestations of evil, demonic possession begins with sin. Sin is what grants Satan access to us. This has been true since the fall of Adam and Eve. Theoretically, if we never sinned then Satan would have no influence or effect upon us. This, however, due to the fall and our resulting sin nature, is not the case.

It is when we surrender to temptation and engage in sin that we open the door for further demonic influence. The demons are the ones who attack and tempt God's people. When we choose Christ and refuse sin, we are, in a manner of speaking, shutting the demonic door. When we choose sin, we are opening the door a bit further each time. The more open the door becomes, the harder it is to close.

Possession is the full-blown opening of the demonic door. Prior to this, there is a struggle of good versus evil, in which the person maintains some of his or her identity and still clings to bits and pieces of desire for good. Eventually overcome by their own sin, the possessed person surrenders control to Satan, and the demons take over. The demons, whose intent is always to steal, kill, and destroy, make the possessed person's intent the same.

This means that in addition to having self-destructive tendencies, the demons use the possessed person to attack others. The possessed person becomes what is known as an agent. Satan uses the agents to identify weak areas in selected threats. These threats can be successful churches, ministers, leaders, etc.

Satan will send whatever number of agents and demons are required to identify these weak areas. These agents and demons will follow, observe, and define the problem areas in Christian leaders. The demons then inform the agents as to the best problem areas to attack. During these attacks, the demons can choose to remain invisible, or they can choose to present themselves in visible form. Visible forms can range from appearing as frightening creatures to appearing as a person. Let's look now at an example of how something like this might play out.

Let's say that some demons and/or agents identify a weak area in the life of a leader in a thriving church. This weakness is an attraction to women to whom he is not married. A plan will then be put into place as to how to lure him into sinning in this area. Satan could then send an attractive female agent or demon disguised as a beautiful woman into the church to begin the seductive process.

The agent or the demon might sit on the front row in revealing clothes during a service. This would likely attract attention, create desire, and open the door for sinful action. She might then do something to become more involved, such as join the choir or get a job at the church. She would eventually make it known that she wanted to get to know him better and try to spend personal time with him. They eventually spend time together, and he ends up having an affair, which continues.

The church eventually finds out about it, and the church leader is dismissed. This could potentially cause his marriage and family to break apart, make it difficult for him to find employment, and/or cause his church members to backslide. The church and its members would likely be heavily affected by this, and the church could potentially dismantle or at least enter a lengthy time of confusion, disappointment, and ineffectiveness. It would seem that Satan's plan was effective.

While this is just an example, it is not something that is entirely uncommon. These types of issues plague churches and Christians across the world, and Satan uses possessed people (agents) to accomplish these tasks. It is also worth noting that you don't have to be a church leader to be the object of demonic attack. Satan wants to keep all people from God. This is just an example of the process by which it happens. The same process could be true of someone in a different vocational setting. It doesn't have to be someone in the ministry; however, Satan often chooses to make the Church his primary target.

This is because, again, Satan's intent is to steal, kill, and destroy and thereby thwart God's plans. So it makes sense that he would attack the very institution that God has established to carry out His work here on the earth, His Church. In Satan's mind, the more people he can possess, the more he can keep from God. Satan thinks that if this is accomplished quickly, he may be able to frustrate God and win the spiritual war. While this may be true theoretically, the foundation of God's Church is built upon Jesus Christ and is unshakeable. Satan is already a defeated foe. It is, however, the Christian's responsibility to be vigilant and aware of these demonic attacks in order to effectively engage in the spiritual battle at hand. Fortunately, for the believer in Christ, he or she has been given power and access to the resources of the Kingdom of God, which far outweigh those of the kingdom of darkness.

chapter fifteen:
power of the christian

To use a cliché, there are two sides to the coin. We've talked extensively about Satan, demons, and the ways in which they can affect our lives and the world around us. This kingdom of darkness is one side of the coin. The kingdom of light, God's Kingdom, is the other. The powers of the Kingdom of God far outweigh those of the kingdom of darkness. When Christians access this power, miracles occur, evil is defeated, and victorious lives are lived.

The power of the Christian centers wholly on Jesus Christ. While it is true that the Holy Spirit is the giver of this power, Jesus made this available to us. If you recall in the opening chapter of this section, we talked about Jesus's life, death, and resurrection and the significance of this for the believer. I ended that section by talking about how the Holy Spirit indwells that person and seals him or her in the Lord.

In this chapter, we will go a step further and look at how the Holy Spirit empowers the believer in Christ. We've talked about Satan and his demons and their influence upon the world. They, however, cannot stand in the presence of the power of God. In fact, they have absolutely no power in the presence of God. Satan is already a defeated foe, and he and his demons flee at the name of Jesus. The reason we do not experience this reality as often as we should is because, particularly in affluent societies, it has become increasingly rare that Christians access the fullness of the power of the Holy Spirit given to them by Christ. Surrounded by wealth and modern convenience, the need for the Holy Spirit in one's daily life is often overlooked.

In addition to not fully taking advantage of the gift of the Holy Spirit, there are other weapons God has given us to fight the enemy that often go overlooked. God has given us His Word (the Bible), the name of Jesus, the blood of Jesus, prayer, fasting, and the Church. These weapons empower us to defeat the kingdom of darkness. In this chapter, we'll look at the role that each of these plays and discuss what it looks like to pursue and access each one. We'll begin with the Holy Spirit.

HOLY SPIRIT

Following His ascension into heaven after His resurrection, Jesus poured out the Holy Spirit upon mankind, specifically on those who were together waiting on Him, and thus began the start of the Christian church. We find the account of this in Acts 2. On the day of Pentecost, a group of Jesus's followers was together awaiting the arrival of the Holy Spirit that Jesus promised to them in Acts 1. While they were together, there "came a sound from heaven, as of a rushing mighty wind, and it filled the whole house where they were sitting" (2:2). They then "began to speak with other tongues, as the Spirit gave them utterance" (2:4). This led to others around them taking notice because they heard them speaking about God in their various languages, which "amazed and perplexed" them (v. 12). Peter, filled with the Holy Spirit, began to preach, and around three thousand were saved following the sermon.

We then are given the account of what the time following Pentecost looked like for those who had believed upon Christ. This account is found in Acts 2:42–47, but I will give some highlights here. Verse 43 says that "fear came upon every soul, and many wonders and signs were done through the apostles." Verse 45 tells us that they "sold their possessions and goods, and divided them among all, as anyone had need." Verse 47 closes out the chapter, saying that "the Lord added to the church daily those who were being saved." (2:47).

So in summary, there are clearly some very important things that happen when believers allow the Holy Spirit to take over in their lives. The most significant is that people are saved. This is made clear by the fact that three thousand were saved after Peter preached. Not only this, but God continued to add to that number "daily." If we want to be most effective in winning souls for the Kingdom of God and thereby thwarting Satan's attempts at dismantling God's plan, then we must rely on the Holy Spirit's presence, power, and guidance. Nowhere in Acts 2 is there any mention of demonic interference. I believe that this is because the presence of the Holy Spirit was so strong that the powers of darkness could not interfere.

The next important takeaway is that reliance on the Holy Spirit leads to Godly fellowship with others. We'll get into this more when we talk about the importance of the church, but I'll mention here that relationships centered on the Holy Spirit produce fruitful outcomes. Strong Christian fellowship is essential in the fight against the enemy.

Like God the Father and God the Son, the Holy Spirit is all knowing, all powerful, and omnipresent. He works to guide, help, teach, train, and work with Christians. In so doing, He enables believers to overcome their demonic enemies. He does this by revealing the schemes of the enemy and revealing to believers how to defeat and destroy these schemes through the gifts of the Holy Spirit (1 Cor. 12). He also helps believers pray according to the will of God (Romans 8:26).

Now, having established that the Holy Spirit is the primary source of power in the Christian's life, let's look at some of the other weapons God has given us to defeat the schemes of the enemy. As I discuss these Christian resources, you will notice that none stand independent of one another. They are all interconnected. In other words, to live truly victorious lives in Christ we must not merely focus on one area and leave the rest unattended. They all work together and serve specific purposes and must be used accordingly.

THE NAME OF JESUS

All the power of God is wrapped up and invested in the name of Jesus. For starters, salvation exists solely in Jesus Christ. Acts 4:12 tells us that there is not "salvation in any other, for there is no other name under heaven given among men by which we must be saved." Without salvation, no one has power in this life. Any and all who are not saved are easy targets for demonic oppression. With salvation comes power, and this salvation is only attained through Jesus Christ and confessing Him as Lord and Savior. Romans 10:9 tells us that if we "confess with [our] mouth the Lord Jesus and believe in [our] heart that God has raised him from the dead, [we] will be saved." Once this strength is attained through salvation, we only gain further ability to access the power of the name of Jesus.

One of these powers deals specifically with authority over the enemy. When we are saved and filled with the Holy Spirit, we inherit the power that Jesus had while on earth and still has today. In fact, Jesus tells us in John 14:12 that we will do even "greater works" than He by the power of His name. This means that we are given complete authority over the enemy. Complete authority means that when we speak the name of Jesus, the enemy loses its power. Philippians 2:10 tells us "that at the name of Jesus every knee should bow, of those in heaven, and of those on earth, and of those under the earth."

Jesus's name carries all power and authority both in the earthly realm and the spiritual realm. Demons have to flee because they cannot stand in the presence of the name of Jesus.

What this means for Christians is that they have the ability to drive out demons when they engage in the battle with faith. We have been given power to move mountains when we approach issues with strong and sincere faith (Mark 11:23–24). Having authority to drive out demons means that we also have power over the afflictions that they cause. When we command demons to leave with sincere faith and confidence in the name of Jesus, they must leave along with the problems that they cause.

THE BLOOD OF JESUS

Working hand in hand with the name of Jesus to give us power is the blood of Jesus. Just as with the name of Jesus, demons fear the blood. When Jesus was crucified, His shed blood defeated the power of sin forever. Sin is of Satan and his kingdom, so this means that the blood of Jesus defeated Satan forever. Satan, demons, sickness, disease, and all other problems fear the blood.

The power of the blood of Jesus Christ is still alive today. It speaks to the Father saying that we are redeemed and alive in Christ (Heb. 12:24). Christians are covered by the blood of Jesus from the day they surrender their lives to Christ. When a demon looks at a believer covered in the blood, he sees Jesus rather than that person. Demons flee from Jesus; thus, they flee from Christians.

Experiencing the power of the blood of Jesus does not come so much by active engagement as much as it does by remembrance and realization. Christians are covered fully by the blood of Jesus at the moment of salvation. This does not change from day to day. We gain power and confidence through realizing this truth, and it emboldens us to engage more fully the other spiritual weapons we have. For example, when we realize that demons flee from the homes of believers because they see the homes covered in blood, we realize more fully the blood's power and can walk more confidently in a Spirit-led life.

THE WORD OF GOD

The reason other Christians and I know these things to be true, aside from personal experience, is because of the Word of God. Also known as the Bible, the

Word of God is the final and comprehensive collection of God's teachings to mankind. Within His Word are the history and origin of the world and mankind, the fall of man into sin, the gospel message of salvation to those who believe upon Christ, and God's ultimate plan of redemption for the world and those who believe upon Him. The Bible demonstrates these overarching themes through historical accounts of individuals and societies that once inhabited the earth.

The Old Testament, while pointing to Jesus Christ, covers the time before Christ came to the earth. The New Testament begins with the four books that are known as the "Gospels." Made up of Matthew, Mark, Luke, and John, these books detail the life of Jesus Christ, His teachings, and finally His death, resurrection, and ascension into heaven. The fifth book, Acts, deals largely with the formation of the Christian church. The rest of the New Testament, written in the form of letters, serves primarily as an instructional manual for how to live the Christian life, with the book of Revelation ending the Bible and dealing with the End Times.

The Word of God, although written by men, is completely inspired by God. This means that it is not man's words with God's approval but instead God's words breathed out and written by the hands of men. It is, therefore, free of error and to be held in the highest regard.

God's Word is powerful and has the ability to protect us, which is why it is a spiritual weapon. Hebrews 4:12 tells us that "the word of God is living and powerful, and sharper than any two-edged sword, piercing even to the division of soul and spirit, and of joints and marrow, and is a discerner of the thoughts and intents of the heart." So here, one way that the Word of God serves as a source of protection is because it penetrates not only our physical being ("joints and marrow") but also our inner spiritual being ("soul and spirit"). This means that the Word of God has the power to convict every part of who we are. When God uses His Word to accomplish this, we become stronger in our fight against the devil and his schemes and become more like Christ.

Similar to prayer, we accomplish this by engaging in the process of reading the Bible, studying it, memorizing scripture, and asking God to guide us and teach us in our study. When we do this, the Holy Spirit will illuminate passages of scripture that teach us, encourage us, convict us, and ultimately grow and strengthen us in our faith.

THE POWER IN GOD'S WORD

There is power in God's Word for several reasons. For starters, He used His Word to speak creation into being. With His Word, He created from nothing. This means that His Word contains His intent, His power, and everything else needed to achieve His purpose. There is power in this purpose. We see this in creation. He intentionally created man and everything else in the world to adopt certain roles and serve certain purposes. There was also clearly power in His Word due to the action that took place when He spoke it. He did not have to repeat Himself, and He did not have to wait for the desired result. He spoke, and it happened.

Additionally, Jesus used the spoken word to proclaim the message of salvation when He preached. He also used the spoken word to heal people and cast out demons. We now have the Word of God and all the power therein to speak over situations. God's Word is a reflection of Himself because it originated from within Him. God is powerful; thus, His Word is powerful. God is also alive and active. Therefore, when we speak His Word, it too is alive and active.

ABIDING IN THE WORD

How, then, do we place ourselves in a position to both experience and activate the power of God's Word? First, we abide in it. Then, we speak it. To abide in something is both to act according to it and to continually remain in it. There is a theme throughout Scripture that if we abide in God's Word, bearing fruit follows. By bearing fruit, I mean that we experience victory over sin, increased effectiveness in ministry, and a deeper, more fulfilling relationship with Christ. Consider the following passages of Scripture that talk about abiding in God and in His Word. Remember that John 1:1 tells us that the "Word was God," so to abide in God is to abide in the Word, and to abide in the Word is to abide in God.

1. John 8:31: Then Jesus said to those Jews who believed Him, "If you abide in My word, you are My disciples indeed.

2. John 10:28–29: And I give them eternal life, and they shall never perish; neither shall anyone snatch them out of My hand. My Father, who has given them to Me, is greater than all; and no one is able to snatch them out of My Father's hand.

3. John 15:4–5: Abide in Me, and I in you. As the branch cannot

bear fruit of itself, unless it abides in the vine, neither can you, unless you abide in Me.

"I am the vine, you are the branches. He who abides in Me, and I in him, bears much fruit; for without Me you can do nothing.

4. John 15:10: If you keep My commandments, you will abide in My love, just as I have kept My Father's commandments and abide in His love.

5. 1 John 3:6: Whoever abides in Him does not sin. Whoever sins has neither seen Him nor known Him.

6. 1 John 3:24: Now he who keeps His commandments abides in Him, and He in him. And by this we know that He abides in us, by the Spirit whom He has given us.

7. 1 John 4:13: By this we know that we abide in Him, and He in us, because He has given us of His Spirit.

Part of abiding in God's Word is meditating upon it and memorizing it. One of the primary reasons we experience strength when we do this is because it allows us to discern the devil's lies. The essence of Satan's temptation is deception. We see this from the beginning when he twisted God's words in the Garden of Eden when tempting Eve. Consider the beginning of Genesis 3, which documents the fall:

> Now the serpent was more cunning than any beast of the field which the LORD God had made. And he said to the woman, "Has God indeed said, 'You shall not eat of every tree of the garden'?"

> And the woman said to the serpent, "We may eat the fruit of the trees of the garden; but of the fruit of the tree which is in the midst of the garden, God has said, 'You shall not eat it, nor shall you touch it, lest you die.'"

> Then the serpent said to the woman, "You will not surely die. For God knows that in the day you eat of it your eyes will be opened, and you will be like God, knowing good and evil.

Satan twisted God's Word and lured Eve into sin. It was not a blatant, bold "I want you to go directly against what God said" approach. It was a "did God really say that" approach. This method leaves room for interpretation in the mind when not immediately met with God's truth, and this can lead to justification. Eve fell into this trap. She interpreted both God's Word and the serpent's and then justified eating the fruit. Verse 6 tells us that she "saw that the tree was good for food, that it was pleasant to the eyes, and a tree desirable to make one wise" (Gen. 3:6). So she ate.

Jesus serves as the greatest example of what it means to know the Word, speak the Word, and defeat the tactics of the enemy. Matthew 4:1–11 details the account of the temptation of Jesus in the wilderness. Consider this passage:

> Then Jesus was led up by the Spirit into the wilderness to be tempted by the devil. And when He had fasted forty days and forty nights, afterward He was hungry. Now when the tempter came to Him, he said, "If You are the Son of God, command that these stones become bread."

> But He answered and said, "It is written, 'Man shall not live by bread alone, but by every word that proceeds from the mouth of God.'"

> Then the devil took Him up into the holy city, set Him on the pinnacle of the temple, and said to Him, "If You are the Son of God, throw Yourself down. For it is written:

> 'He shall give His angels charge over you,' and, 'In their hands they shall bear you up, Lest you dash your foot against a stone.'"

> Jesus said to him, "It is written again, 'You shall not tempt the LORD your God.'"

> Again, the devil took Him up on an exceedingly high mountain, and showed Him all the kingdoms of the world and their glory. And he said to Him, "All these things I will give You if You will fall down and worship me."

Then Jesus said to him, "Away with you, Satan! For it is written, 'You shall worship the LORD your God, and Him only you shall serve.'"

Then the devil left Him, and behold, angels came and ministered to Him.

Here, Satan not only twists God's Word, but uses it. Satan directly quotes Scripture in verse 6. Jesus, however, leaves no room for interpretation or justification. He immediately responds with Scripture, and what does the devil do? He moves on and attempts to defeat Jesus in another area. He knows he cannot win in the presence of strong scriptural knowledge. When Jesus says in verse 7, "It is written again, 'You shall not tempt the Lord your God,'" Satan moves on because he cannot win when one's defense rests in the truth of God's Word. The devil's primary tactic of temptation is looking for a weak spot where he could make us believe a lie. When we speak Scripture, we crush the lie. Satan's lies cannot stand in the power of God's truth when we speak it.

Notice also Jesus's ability to immediately speak Scripture. He leaves no room for temptation to blossom. Jesus shoots it down instantly. This is where memorizing Scripture becomes so important. The more we meditate upon it and memorize it, the easier it is to trample the lies of the enemy, regardless of the situation. The more we root ourselves in the Word of God and memorize what it says, the more we are reminded of His unchanging Truth. The more deeply rooted we are in the Truth, the more able we are to recognize and defeat the lies of the enemy. When we combine the knowledge of the Word of God with the speaking of the Word of God, we experience the inherent power that it contains, a power that is "living and powerful, and sharper than any two-edged sword" (Heb. 4:12).

THE CHURCH

One of God's greatest gifts to His people is the church. A tangible representation of His dedication to His people, the church is evidence that the Christian life is not meant to be lived alone. Although spending time alone with God is certainly important, so is spending time with His people. A spirit-filled church offers a place for God's people to worship, receive Bible teaching, and fellowship with others. It also provides believers with opportunities to do the ministry that Jesus calls them to do in the Great Commission found in Matthew 28:19–20.

One thing that is particularly significant about the church is the mutual benefit that exists for both the believers and for the communities that the churches serve. In other words, the more the individuals in a church benefit from its teaching, fellowship, etc., the more the community benefits. For example, when a believer receives strong, true biblical teaching, that often leads him or her to a greater understanding of his or her purpose on the earth. This, in turn, will often lead to a greater desire to carry out that purpose and seek God and minister to those around them with greater passion and urgency. When this is combined with the encouragement and accountability that comes through corporate worship and fellowship, the believer is more likely to stay the course and engage in a lifestyle of ministry and service to God for the long haul. When this happens, people are led to Christ. When people are led to Christ, communities change.

It is based on the simple premise of light driving out darkness. Communities with no strong Christian churches are consumed by darkness. The nonbelievers living there are walking blindly and living lives that reflect that blindness. One will often find these communities severely afflicted by poverty, violence, disease, broken family structures, and so on. When a strong Christian church emerges in a community, and people begin to come to know Christ, they are moved from a mentality of darkness into one of light.

In order to reap the spiritual benefits that God extends to us through His church, it is vital that we invest our time, resources, and relational energy into it. Think of a gym membership. A gym is somewhere that people go to get stronger. Whether it's swimming, lifting weights, running, or playing sports, the goal of exercise is to improve the body and, often, the mind as well. A major reason people join gyms is because gyms provide all the equipment needed to make all parts of the body strong. However, if people with memberships never go to the gym to work out, they won't get any stronger because they are not using the equipment available.

How we decide to interact with the church is very similar. God has given us a place to experience fellowship, accountability, Bible teaching, corporate worship, ministry, and the spiritual empowerment that comes with these gifts. If we do not choose to access them, however, then we will not experience the blessing and growth that they offer. The formation of the Christian church did not happen by accident. It was an intentional gift from God designed to build His kingdom on Earth and strengthen His people. For both our personal benefit and the expansion of His kingdom, we must dutifully and intentionally make investing in the church a central part of our lives.

chapter sixteen: prayer

The importance of prayer in one's spiritual walk cannot go understated. It is, at its core, a discipline of dependence. It is a discipline in the sense that it is ongoing and requires some effort and is dependent in the sense that it acknowledges our dependence on God. Whether we realize it or not, when we prayerfully posture ourselves before God, we are acknowledging that we are not the greatest source of our being and/or circumstance. In other words, we are not our own "end-all-be-all" and are engaging in an act of humility.

There is great power in humility, and Jesus is our greatest example of this. Philippians 2:8 says of Jesus, "And being found in appearance as a man, He humbled Himself and became obedient to the point of death, even the death of the cross." The greatest act of power the world has ever seen, the triumph over sin and death, came through the most humble and selfless act the world has ever known. The God of this world and Creator of all that is in it came to this world in the form of a man and died so that we might be saved from sin and brought into new life with Him, both now and eternally. Clearly, there is great power in humility.

Sincere prayer is a humble act, and there is great power in this. When we humble ourselves before God, we place ourselves in a position to be used by God for the glory of His kingdom. When we live a prayer-centered life, we are acknowledging daily that we need God. Whether it be our circumstance, our relationships, or our fight against sin, when we pray we are inviting God to work in the situation.

In addition to the power found in the humility of sincere prayer, there is power in the words that are spoken when we pray. Holy Spirit-led prayers in accord with God's will enact the power of God. Our prayers enact the power of the weapons we've talked about thus far: the name of Jesus, the blood of Jesus, and the Word of God.

WHAT SINCERE PRAYER IS NOT

Before getting into how our prayers call to action the power of God, we need to establish what sincere prayer is versus what it is not. Many people approach prayer from what I will call a "genie-in-a-bottle" approach. What I mean by this is that they tend to only pray when they need something that they feel will benefit them. For example, they may pray for a promotion at work or for their favorite team to win a big game. While it is not wrong to ask for things from the Lord, this approach tends to be self-centered and self-serving. This can so often lead to believing that God exists primarily to improve our earthly circumstance, rather than existing to save our souls and protect us from the enemy. Again, this is not to say that God requires that His people live in misery. God is a good God and gives good gifts (Matt. 7:11, James 1:17). It's just that He is more concerned with the salvation of His people and the life-giving relationship that comes as a result of that.

The second approach is one of duty. Falling into this category tends to produce a rather dull prayer life because we approach God out of a place of responsibility rather than relationship and conviction. In the same way that asking God for things is not wrong, approaching God out of duty is not inherently wrong. Like I said earlier, there is certainly a component of discipline to a strong prayer life. However, we shouldn't approach prayer from a rigid, get-in-get-out standpoint just because we know that we should pray. God invites us to not merely say words aimed somewhere in His general direction but to experience Him, learn from Him, rest in Him, and receive and be reminded of His grace and mercy.

What, then, does this look like? Jesus gives us a very strong template for what prayer should look like in Matthew 6:9–13:

> Our Father in heaven,
> Hallowed be Your name.
> Your kingdom come.
> Your will be done
> On earth as it is in heaven.
> Give us this day our daily bread.
> And forgive us our debts,
> As we forgive our debtors.
> And do not lead us into temptation,
> But deliver us from the evil one.

For Yours is the kingdom and the power and the glory forever.
Amen.

Notice that the prayer opens with acknowledgment of and adoration for God. It then establishes the superiority of God's will and the desire to see it carried out on the earth. It then moves to asking for God to provide for our needs, forgive us, give us the ability to forgive others, and protect us from sin and evil.

Since Jesus both taught us how to pray and prayed Himself, then clearly prayer is and should be an important part of our lives. When we pray, we are demonstrating being made in the image of God. One reason for this is that prayer involves words, and words are the building blocks for creation. Remember, God used the Word to literally speak creation into being. So when we speak and pray, we are reflecting a part of who He is. It is also a reflection of being made in the image of God because Jesus prayed. So if we are imitating Him, we are bearing witness to the fact that we are made in His image.

WHAT SINCERE PRAYER IS

Now that we've looked at what sincere prayer is not, let's look at what it is. As a starting point, consider the following scriptures, some from the Old and some from the New Testament, that talk about prayer:

1. 2 Chronicles 7:14: "If My people who are called by My name will humble themselves, and pray and seek My face, and turn from their wicked ways, then I will hear from heaven, and will forgive their sin and heal their land.

2. Psalm 34:17: "The righteous cry out, and the LORD hears, and delivers them out of all their troubles."

3. Mark 1:35: "Now in the morning, having risen a long while before daylight, He went out and departed to a solitary place; and there He prayed."

4. Luke 11:9: "So I say to you, ask, and it will be given to you; seek, and you will find; knock, and it will be opened to you."

5. John 16:23–24: "And in that day you will ask Me nothing. Most assuredly, I say to you, whatever you ask the Father in My name He will give you. Until now you have asked nothing in My name.

Ask, and you will receive, that your joy may be full."

6. Ephesians 6:18: "Praying always with all prayer and supplication in the Spirit."

7. James 5:16: "Confess your trespasses to one another, and pray for one another, that you may be healed. The effective, fervent prayer of a righteous man avails much."

One quality of sincere prayer made clear by these scriptures is that sincere prayer is intentional. When we engage with God in prayer in an intentional way, He shows up. Consider Mark 1:35. This verse, speaking about Jesus, tells of a specific instance where He prayed. He got up "a long while before daylight" and went to a remote place to pray alone. It is not an act that He engages in passively. He takes steps to make it a reverent, intentional time.

The next verses give us some insight into why He likely went to pray. When the disciples noticed He was away, they went looking for Him. When they found Him, He told them it was time to go on to the next town and preach (v. 38). It seems here that Jesus went away seeking guidance and fellowship with the Father, received just that, and came back rejuvenated and ready to continue the journey. When we do things like get up early and take time to be alone with God, we are much more likely to draw near to Him because we are placing ourselves in a position to experience Him.

Sincere prayer is also humble. One thing that is consistent with prayer throughout the Bible is that the prayers of the righteous are effective. Christians are made righteous before God by the blood of Jesus. Although we are declared righteous before God through Jesus, the process of becoming holy and more Christlike is ongoing. This process is known as sanctification. One quality of a righteous life is that it is one lived with humility. So when the righteous pray, as mentioned in James 5:16 and Psalm 34:17, they humbly submit themselves before God. Going back to the Lord's Prayer, we see this theme of humility within those lines. Consider the following:

> Give us this day our daily bread.
> And forgive us our debts,
> As we forgive our debtors.
> And do not lead us into temptation,
> But deliver us from the evil one.

The very fact that we are instructed to pray like this means that in order to approach God with our pleas, we need to do it humbly. For the one praying this prayer, these lines establish that we need God to provide for our physical needs (v. 11), forgive us our sins (v. 12), and work on our behalf in the fight against evil (v. 13). Even if not said explicitly, what is being expressed is that we are not our own Savior. We are acknowledging that we need God to intervene in our lives because we cannot do it on our own. When we do this from a truly humble place, we, figuratively speaking, place God in His rightful place as God of our lives, therefore allowing Him to work freely and powerfully on our behalf.

While there are many qualities of sincere prayer that we could discuss, the last one we will focus on is that sincere prayer is confident. Look back at Luke 11:9 and John 16:23–24. These verses do not say, "Ask, and it may be given to you." They also do not say, "Feel free to ask, but no guarantees." No, Luke 11:9 tells us that if we ask, "It will be given." John 16:23 tells us that if we ask in Jesus's name, it will be given to us.

Like praying humbly, praying confidently is another way that we figuratively place God in His rightful position as God of our lives. When we pray in confidence, we are acknowledging that He is the source of power and blessing in our lives, not us. We are also declaring that He is able to answer our requests, even those which seem impossible (Luke 1:37).

THE RESULT OF SINCERE PRAYER

Now that we've looked at what sincere prayer is, let's look at what happens when we pray in this way. In short, it works. There is overwhelming power in the name of Jesus, the blood of Jesus, and the Word of God, and when we pray "always...in the Spirit," we enact and experience the power of these weapons in our lives and in the world around us (Ephesians 6:18, James 5:16). In this section, we'll look at how prayer provides us power that leads to protection, intimacy with God, and access to One who works as an intercessor for us.

POWER TO PROTECTION

When we pray in the Spirit, we experience power, and this power leads to protection. Why is this though? Let's start with a simple example. We have already talked about the process of how sin works, but as a brief refresher: our sin nature combined with demonic influence leads to temptation, which encourages us to sin. Without salvation in Jesus Christ and the working of the Holy Spirit, we are bound by and enslaved to those sinful desires. When we are saved, however, we are united with Christ, filled with the Holy Spirit, and our inner man is changed from a nature of sin to the nature of Christ. However, this does not mean that we are free from the struggle against sin. Fighting sin is exactly that: a fight. The Christian life is not something that is passive in nature.

Think of it like this. Say you have a plant that is dying and withering away. This is us before salvation. You notice that the plant is dying, so you give it water and, thereby, save the plant. Think of this as a parallel to salvation and being filled with the Holy Spirit. If the plant, however, does not continue to receive water and sunlight and the other things necessary to sustain its life, what happens? It eventually withers away and dies. Now, I know that this example is not exactly the same as the Christian life because the plant is not actively doing anything to receive the life-giving water, but the general principle of needing to be continuously filled and refreshed is the same.

Similarly, Christians need to continually receive renewal and refreshment in the Spirit, and a primary way that we experience that is through prayer. When we are saved, it does not mean that we will never fall into sin again; it means that we now have the capacity to overcome sins we once struggled with or didn't even recognize and, thereby, live in obedience to God in a way that we couldn't before salvation. When we do fall into sin, however, it chips away at the light within us. Therefore, it is vital that we continually seek God and the refreshing of the Holy Spirit to live a holy and victorious life.

So let's look at how prayer helps us achieve this. Before salvation, when one is struck with an unholy thought that leads to fleshly desire and then to sin, they do not recognize this as sinful. Some may realize that it is morally questionable, but they do not recognize it as sinful. After salvation, we are able to discern these desires. So when Christians experience these thoughts and desires and recognize them as ones that will lead to sin if unchecked, we are to go to God in prayer. When we confess these concerns in the name of Jesus Christ and bind the demons causing the thoughts and desires, we take away their power. To bind something is to tie it up and restrain it. For example, when a law enforcement officer binds a criminal's wrists with handcuffs, it largely removes the criminal's ability to use their hands to fight back. This is effectively what we are doing when we pray in the name of Jesus.

Once this prayerful process is started, we are to cast the demons out (command them to leave) and plead that the blood of Jesus Christ cover our mind, will, and emotions. We then should begin to meditate upon the goodness of the Lord. As we continue in this process, we will be set free from the temptation (2 Cor. 10:5).

This process applies to all issues that demons cause, whether it be individually sinful actions, sickness, conflict with others, etc. Demons have to flee at the name of Jesus, and if they have to flee, then so do the problems.

INTIMACY

Another result of sincere prayer is intimacy with God. If demonic influence leads to temptation and sin, and sin to separation from God, then praying in a way that causes victory over demonic influence and sin can only lead to greater intimacy with God. To be clear, when I say separation from God, I do not mean separation in the sense of a loss of salvation. I mean it in the sense of us not experiencing the joy and peace and victory that results from fellowship with Christ.

One of the beauties and mysteries of the gospel message is that God not only allows us to have a relationship with Him, He desires it. He wants us to know Him intimately and live victoriously as a result. Think about some of your closest friends. I would imagine that those relationships exist because you both know each other deeply. You probably enjoy them, trust them, and depend on them for things, and reaching this level of relationship with them was likely attained by spending a lot of time together.

At a basic level, prayer is spending time with God. It is talking to Him, listening to Him, and getting to know Him better. The more we do this, the better we get to know Him. To use the friendship analogy, think about how you normally feel around your close friends. I would imagine that you are probably pretty comfortable around them because you are able to be yourself. Now, think about how you act as a result. Because you know them so well and they you, you are probably honest with them and likely don't want to do anything that will disappoint them or negatively affect the relationship. The same can be said about our relationship with God. The more we know Him, the more we realize His great love for us and the less we want to do anything that would negatively affect our fellowship with Him (sin). One of the primary ways we reach this level of intimacy and fellowship with God is through spending time with Him in prayer.

INTERCESSION

The last result of sincere prayer that we will talk about in this chapter is intercession. What this means is that when we pray, the Holy Spirit intervenes on our behalf. So these spiritual weapons we've talked about—the name of Jesus, the blood of Jesus, and the Holy Spirit—come to engage in the spiritual war for us. Romans 8:26–27 makes clear how the Holy Spirit responds to our prayers. These verses state,

> Likewise the Spirit also helps in our weaknesses. For we do not know what we should pray for as we ought, but the Spirit Himself makes intercession for us with groanings which cannot be uttered. Now He who searches the hearts knows what the mind of the Spirit is, because He makes intercession for the saints according to the will of God.

To intercede is to act on behalf of someone else. So an intercessor would be the one who intercedes. In the case of us when we pray, the Holy Spirit is our intercessor.

This is a profound and empowering truth. What these verses tell us is that we do not have to have everything figured out or be right about everything for the Holy Spirit to act on our behalf. We just need to engage in the process of prayer, and when we do, the greatest power the world has ever known comes to work on our behalf. This means that when we pray for provision, healing, guidance, strength against temptation—whatever it may be—we are met with the provision, healing, guidance, strength, etc. of the Holy Spirit. We can also rest in the fact that this intercession is always for our good. Romans 8:28 tells us that "all things work together for good to those who love God, to those who are the called according to His purpose." Not only does the Holy Spirit act on our behalf when we pray, He acts in our interest.

TEMPLATE/EXAMPLE PRAYER

So we have established what sincere prayer is not, what sincere prayer is, and what happens when we earnestly seek God through prayer. If all of this information seems overwhelming, don't worry. We will tie it all together here. In this section I will give a sample prayer that you can use as a template for your own prayer life and discuss how it encompasses what we have talked about in this chapter. For this example, we will look at a prayer for healing. I will give numbered points that will serve as an instructional basis and then discuss what it looks like to practically carry that out.

1. Acknowledge that God is the awesome and loving Father who gives all good gifts.

   Just as with Jesus's instructions on how to pray in Matthew 6, we too begin with praise and adoration for the Father. By doing this, we are acknowledging that regardless of circumstance or outcome, God is still good and still in control. We are humbly expressing that we are not our own savior, and we are inviting the Holy Spirit to step in and intercede on our behalf.

2. Remember and assert that Satan is both the father of all lies and the source of all evil.

   Here, we are speaking words against Satan and evil, thereby reminding him that he is a defeated foe and has no power or authority over us because we are children of God. We are commanding Satan, his demons, and the problems they are causing to leave.

3. Remember that Jesus took all our sins upon Himself.

   When we do this, we are reminding ourselves of the ultimate sacrifice and victory that triumphs over any circumstance, and that is the life, death, and resurrection of Jesus Christ.

4. Command the desired outcome.

   In this stage of prayer, we are using assertive language and speaking directly to the issue at hand. By doing this, we are exercising our God-given authority over evil through the power of Jesus Christ and the Holy Spirit.

SAMPLE PRAYER

Let's consider what this might look like using the example of prayer for healing. I will break it up into sections and number them so that it is easy to identify which of the four parts is being covered.

1. Dear Heavenly Father, thank you so much for this day and what you are doing for me and through me. I come to you before your throne of grace that you may grant me mercy because I am needy, and you understand very well my circumstances. Thank you for all of the many blessings you have poured out upon me.

2. Devil, you are a liar. I am not sick. You are lying to me with these symptoms. I declare to you that you are a defeated foe. You are fallen, powerless, and miserable. Right now, I speak to you that whatever you are causing me to go through is a lie. The Word of my Father tells me that I am more than a conqueror (Romans 8:37). I am above, not under; I am a head and not a tail. By His stripes, I was and am healed. Therefore, I command you and all your demons of (name of disease) to pack up your evil deeds (related to the problem) and go and never come back in Jesus's name.

3. Lord Jesus, I give you all the praise. Thank you for loving me so much that you took my place so that all my sins and the resulting consequences were put on you (1 Peter 2:24). You became a ransom for me. You saved me from my sins, and I give You all the praise and glory.

4. My body, I speak to you. Be healed in the name of Jesus! You are the temple of the Most High God (1 Corinthians 6:19), where the Holy Spirit dwells. Now, be healed in Jesus's name.

While this is an example of prayer in the instance of physical healing, you can use this as a template for prayer in any area. This includes prayers for strength, guidance, provision, protection, wisdom, etc. God enjoys hearing our requests and invites us to experience Him and His great power through entering into His presence in prayer (Matt. 7:7–11). To God be the glory, and may He guide you in your prayerful pursuit of Him.

chapter seventeen:
human spirit/soul/body

As you know, one of the primary intents of this book is to promote and develop not only an awareness of the spiritual realm, but an understanding of it. Furthermore, I want you to understand how our decisions contribute to how we interact with the spiritual realm. We talked about how sin works in the Satan chapter, but we are going to take a deeper look at how the human spirit, soul, and body work together to influence the choices we make. One of the main intents of this chapter is to make you aware of both how the subconscious affects our choices and how our choices affect the subconscious. It may seem a bit confusing now, but hopefully by the end of the chapter you will come to a greater understanding of how we make choices, which will hopefully contribute in a positive way to the choices that you make.

Because many likely think of personhood as primarily existing in the physical body, we will begin there. The body can be defined as the physical housing unit of man and woman. It is composed of the flesh and blood that make up our interior and exterior body parts and bodily systems. All of these structures and systems provide a vehicle for us to accomplish selected tasks and move around in the world. The body is an obedient instrument; it does not make decisions on its own. It responds to the soul.

Every person is a human-spirit being. God created man with the capacity to receive information directly from Him. He also gave him the ability to know and understand this information, which is intended to guide the soul and lead it in making decisions that align with the will of God. The human spirit accomplishes this by helping the soul discern evil and selfish thoughts and plans that are not from God.

God is also a Spirit being and assigns the Holy Spirit to interact with and guide us. Man was created to be completely in accord with God. This meant, before the fall, that we would always make the choices He intended for us to make. Had this stayed the case, our choices would have always been ones of purity, love, and selflessness. However, after man's fall into sin in the Garden of Eden, we were corrupted and turned into people that no longer naturally desired the things/will of God. When this happened, man began to desire sinful things, and a whole new realm of spiritual input became a reality. Now, we are caught in a battle of spiritual input from God and spiritual input from Satan. This is why it is so important that we learn to distinguish between the two. We have the choice to accept or reject the Holy Spirit's guidance, but rejection will lead to detrimental consequences.

The third part of our being is the human soul. Think of the soul as the personality center of man. A soul is comprised of three parts: the mind, the will, and the emotions. The mind is where good and evil thoughts are generated. When we are born, we have an empty mind, meaning we have no thoughts. However, the mind's capacity to generate thoughts leads us to reason and debate, which leads to the making of decisions. The will then becomes involved because the will is where decisions are made. The repetition of this process over time leads to the development of personality traits, which result from the manifestation of our emotions (anger, sympathy, sadness, excitement, enjoyment, etc.).

The reason our personalities exist in our souls is because the way we feel about something often derives from the external input we receive from the five senses (sight, touch, smell, taste, and hearing). God placed the five senses within the soul to stimulate the mind to generate thoughts and gather information from external sources. Whatever you know and/or believe to be true you either saw, heard, smelled, tasted, or felt. These five senses connect our souls to our bodies. In other words, when we experience a soul-residing sensation from one or more of the five senses, we feel it in our physical body. We then react to the sensation and process our response. When this process is repeated enough, we develop personality traits.

For example, let's say that growing up someone experiences repeatedly being spoken to in a way that is harsh and angry. This would certainly involve auditory input, but it would also involve visual input as well. There would be body language and facial expressions that would accompany the angry speech. This would be received by the one at whom it was directed and processed by that person. Once the mind receives and processes it, an emotional response is rendered, and a decision is made as to what to do with this information. The recipient of the anger could decide that any further conflict would only make things worse and retreat, or he or she could decide that if they retreat, this type of thing will only continue to happen and possibly get worse. Herein is where personality traits are born. Out of the situation could either be born a passive or conflictive person depending on the processing.

This, however, goes further than just personality traits. It extends to a point of spiritual significance because with the same process of decision making we choose to either obey the desires of the flesh or the desires of the Holy Spirit. The input that we receive that we must process originates from three different sources:

1. God/His Word
2. Satan/Demons
3. World Sources

To the untrained mind, all of the thoughts seem the same because the mind of the unsaved does not distinguish between sinful and not sinful. In other words, they are just thoughts. For example, the mind of an unsaved person does not recognize lust as sinful. Instead, one sees it as a natural response to something that has been seen or thought. When this is the case, the body is likely to respond in accordance with how the mind processes the thought. If the thought is sinful but is not recognized as sinful, then almost always a sinful action will follow because we are naturally inclined to sin. That is our default mode of operation.

This is why it is vital that Christians strive toward growth in discerning the input that we receive. We must ask ourselves and identify whether the thoughts that we have are from God or from Satan and the world because this is where sin originates. This is how sin occurred in the first place. Adam and Eve were met with external input from Satan in the form of a serpent. They were deceived into not truly recognizing sin and its consequences as such, and a sinful action followed. The only way to discern is by feeding on the Word. Hebrews 4:12 tells us that the Word of God is "a discerner of the thoughts and intents of the heart."

The reason this is so important for the believer is because salvation does not mean that worldly input stops. Feeding on the Word and the indwelling of the Holy Spirit give us the ability to discern, but it does not mean that the enemy gives up on trying to cause us to stumble and make us believe the lie that we can be defeated. It doesn't mean that we quit working to grow to a greater awareness of sin and how to overcome the devil. The enemy still wants to defeat us. Satan still wants to draw us into sin because that is his best effort to thwart God's plan. He knows the pain and consequences that sin brings, and since his agenda is always to steal, kill, and destroy, he is hard at work to tempt us into sin. We are called, however, to continuously pursue a greater knowledge of our Lord Jesus Christ (Phil. 3:10). In this pursuit, there is victory. If you are in Christ, you are victorious, and the devil and his demons are defeated foes. God reigns supreme, and His plans will not be thwarted.

PRACTICAL APPLICATION

How, then, do we engage in this process of recognizing demonic input and overcoming the desire to resort to our old nature? We will explore that in this section. Here, we will look at practical steps that we can take to align our thoughts and actions with those of the Father. It can be done, and it requires active engagement in the pursuit of discipline. To be clear, this is not to be mistaken as works-based salvation. Even our best efforts at discipline and obedience don't save us. Salvation is a gift from God and comes only by grace through faith in His Son Jesus Christ (Ephesians 2:8–10). The pursuit of discipline, rather, should come as a result of this salvation. When people know they are children of God, they do not live holy lives because they want to go to heaven, overcome difficult circumstances, be healed, blessed, etc. They live holy lives because they are children of God.

Recognizing and conquering input that is not from God comes down to training the mind to separate good thoughts from evil ones, and this happens through knowing the truth, earnestly seeking God through His Word, and praying. When we choose to feed ourselves with God's Word, we tend to walk in light and gain understanding and the wisdom of God. This is because God is His Word, so to take in the Word is to take in God. God is completely good and all-knowing, so the more of His wisdom we gain, the more we are able to distinguish good from evil. Not only that, but the more we gain His wisdom, the more we are able to rationalize why we shouldn't sin.

Being able to do this is key. For example, I can recognize that a fire is hot, but if I still choose to touch it, I will get burned. Recognizing sinful thoughts is surely important, but growing in the desire to cut sinful thoughts off at the source and say no to their temptations is where true victory is found. God grants us this ability through His Word. It is a great display of love and mercy that when we earnestly seek God through His Word, He transforms us. He doesn't just allow us to take in words on a page. He meets us there and, by the power of His Holy Spirit, molds us and changes us to be more like Him and, in so doing, gives us the power to overcome the temptations of the world.

To summarize, we are all human-spirit beings that have souls and live in bodies. When our mind receives input from external sources, it processes that input. The will then decides whether it is something that should be acted upon or not, and the soul convinces the body. The body then acts in response. Sin originates in the soul. James 1:14–15 makes this clear. These verses state, "14 But each one is tempted when he is drawn away by his own desires and enticed. 15 Then, when desire has conceived, it gives birth to sin; and sin, when it is full-grown, brings forth death." These verses tell us that there is a progression to sin. It starts with desire. If we can learn to identify and rebuke these desires, we can prevent the body from acting in response.

FASTING

Again, the primary way that we engage in this mental training process is through studying God's Word. With that being said, there are things we can and should do that enhance this growth process. As we've talked about, the three parts of man are all interconnected and work together, and the body always acts in response to our inner desires. What we have not talked about is how routinely placing our body under submission helps to give us power over the mind. In other words, when we intentionally place the body under submission, sinful desires lose much of their power, and it becomes easier to overcome these in the mind.

Fasting, another God-given spiritual weapon, is one of the ways we practice putting the body under submission. Fasting is withholding something from the body that it is used to having for an extended period of time. Most often, fasting is thought of in regards to refraining from eating. In today's world, it could also be considered a fast to remove something like technology from your life for a period of time, but for the intents and purposes here we will focus on it from a food standpoint.

Many people, particularly in affluent societies, are used to eating multiple times a day. Because of technology and the ability to mass produce food, people who have access to such food will often eat whenever they feel hungry. In some cases, it becomes more of a habit than anything else. We are told that in order to perform at our peak we need to consume food multiple times a day. It is also a highly social and cultural practice. In other words, food is something that consumes a lot of time and thought-energy in our lives.

Removing food for a period of time is one of the simplest, yet most powerful things we can do to focus our attention on growing closer to the Lord, if we do it with the right motives. Fasting should be done with the intent of going deeper in one's walk with the Lord. Scripture tells us that it should not be done with the intention of being noticed by others. Matthew 6:16–18 states,

> Moreover, when you fast, do not be like the hypocrites, with a
> sad countenance. For they disfigure their faces that they may
> appear to men to be fasting. Assuredly, I say to you, they have
> their reward. But you, when you fast, anoint your head and
> wash your face, so that you do not appear to men to be fasting,
> but to your Father who is in the secret place; and your Father
> who sees in secret will reward you openly.

This is because, like prayer, fasting is not supposed to be about us. Does it benefit us? Yes, because God chooses to bless us through it, but it is not about us. It is about God and giving Him the devotion He deserves. It is out of His love and mercy that He uses it to draw us to Himself, teach us, and grow us to be more like Him.

The enemy wants to keep us distracted from pursuing God, and one way that he does this can be through routine. To be clear, routine is not bad. Having a routine of getting up early and spending intentional time in God's Word and prayer is a good thing. Having an exercise routine is a good thing. Some aspects of routine, however, can become so important to us that we place them before God. They serve as a source of distraction. For example, one could become so fixated with exercise and body image that the routine of going to the gym becomes something he or she obsesses over and puts before his or her relationship with God.

In the case of eating, we get used to eating regularly, and it becomes a very normal part of our lives. It becomes something we think about frequently and something that we often plan our lives around to an extent. When we remove eating from our daily routine, we are suddenly met with both physical and physiological responses: awareness and desire. We become aware of not eating because we experience the physical sensation of being hungry, and the hunger leads to a desire to eat. It is a sensation that cannot be ignored because we have been designed to eat in order to survive.

It is at this point that the wheels of spiritual development begin turning. When we recognize the awareness of being hungry and the desire to eat, we are to take this to the Lord. The fast is intended to drive us to a greater awareness of our need for the Lord. It serves as a reminder that ultimately God is our provider and sustainer. Every time we think of food or realize hunger during a fast, we are to go to God. We are to pray for strength and revelation and are to thank Him for who He is and what He has done for us.

In addition to serving as a reminder of our need for the Lord, there is also significance in the discipline required to complete a fast. Paul, in 1 Corinthians 9:27, tells us that he disciplines his body and "bring[s] it into subjection" so that he is not disqualified from his preaching. In other words, if we preach and claim to believe the gospel of Christ, but do whatever our flesh desires, there is no validity to our faith. This is because our flesh is inclined to sin. When we are saved, there is a change in our spirit that allows us to direct the flesh to obedience. With that being said, fasting and denying the flesh, although physical in nature, is one way to feed the spirit to push us to greater obedience in Christ. When we fast, we are taking a tangible and practical step to deny our flesh. We are declaring that our body does not control us and that we do indeed have the power in Christ to triumph over sinful, fleshly desires.

In summary, the intentionality and discipline of fasting frees up space for God to work in our lives. It creates a tangible awareness of our need for God and facilitates an inner environment that is conducive to giving us the power to overcome sin. We see it throughout the Bible. It is no coincidence that Jesus fasted during Satan's direct temptation of Him in the desert (Matt. 4:1–2, Luke 4:1–2). He knew the temptation would come, and so He prepared Himself spiritually by placing His body under submission. He withstood the temptation and emerged victorious. His example serves as one for us as well. When we place the body under submission, spiritual awakening and strength follows. It is a practice I participate in, as well as the other pastors that I train, and it is one that I encourage you to practice as well.

epilogue

When I look back on my life, I realize that my tendency was to complain about my circumstances. Whether it was sickness, weakness, poverty, or persecution, my inclination was to ask why I was the one chosen to experience these things. I craved a normal existence. I thought that if things were easy and comfortable I would be satisfied and fulfilled. My God, however, is not a normal God with normal plans. He is a mighty God who has exciting, purposeful plans for those whom He has created and loves. I am no exception, and neither are you.

Although I did not ask to be born black, in Africa, to an impoverished and broken family enslaved to witchcraft, God chose to place me in these circumstances, and He knew what He was doing. I now realize every unfortunate circumstance as a stepping stone to where I am now. These life events have proven my God a trustworthy, faithful, and loving God, and He never acts without intention and purpose. He has used my circumstances to not only bring me into His family but many others into His family as well.

God knows the totality of His plan for humankind on earth. He has assigned each of us a destiny and equipped us with all that we need to accomplish His purpose. We may not fully understand this destiny, but God does. Our role is to submit and respond to His guidance through the Holy Spirit, and He will act accordingly.

I liken it in many ways to the chicken-farming operation. In addition to the ways in which God has used it to tangibly represent His faithfulness, I have also realized many symbolic takeaways that have been impactful in my life. Perhaps the most significant is the fact that the chicken-farming operation represents the purpose often found in a life of submission. It demonstrates in many ways what it looks like to serve under one in whom you trust, even when you are not completely sure what the plan is.

In each chicken-farming operation, there are chickens, a structure in which they are housed, and someone who oversees the operation. The chickens live what would be considered a normal life for a chicken. They eat, sleep, reproduce, lay eggs, etc. They have a provider (the overseer) who takes care of them and holds their life and death in his hands. The chickens grow to trust this overseer, knowing that when he makes his way to their housing unit, it is time to eat. Eventually, when the chicken has served its purpose of laying eggs, it dies and is used for meat.

In many ways, the chicken farm mirrors our lives here on earth. This is true particularly for the Christian. Like the chickens, we have physical boundaries (the earth), live within those boundaries, serve our assigned purpose, and have an overseer (God) in charge of it all. At some point, when we have served our purpose and God sees fit for our time on earth to be done, we cross over from life into death.

I'm not completely sure what goes through the chicken's minds, but I haven't seen anything to indicate that they really know what is going on or what their purpose is. For many on earth, the same is true. It was true for me for a large portion of my life. Before becoming a Christian, I just wandered through life thinking that it happened by chance, and I lived by default as a result. In other words, why not become a witchdoctor? After all, I was born into it. I just lived my life not really questioning what was expected of me. It wasn't until I became a believer that this changed.

The point is that when I look back over the course of my life today, there was always an overseer in control, even when I didn't realize it. Furthermore, I didn't have to realize it for it to be true. It was always true. Once I realized it, however, I submitted to it. The more I submitted to it, the better my life became.

Also, I would imagine that if the chickens could look back over the course of their lives, they would see their purpose and the impact that they had. They would see the people that they fed, perhaps even the lives that they saved by providing nutrition to those in need. Furthermore, they would see that their overseer had this plan in mind from the beginning and that it was a good thing.

I think the same could be said of us. There are lots of things that happen in life that we may not understand or even agree with, but I believe deeply that in hindsight everything will make sense. I've already seen this in my life through my now Christ-shaped worldview. His purpose is clear and makes sense. I know now why I was born into the circumstances in which I was born. I know why my life has unfolded the way that it has. It is so that God could use my story and experiences to impact the world for His glory.

Another thing God has revealed to me through the chicken operation deals with the structure of the chicken houses. As I mentioned earlier, because of their heavy-duty construction, they look like old-fashioned prisons. In one sense, they do represent the prison I once lived in when I was enslaved to the kingdom of darkness. More than that, though, these structures represent freedom and God's faithfulness. The chicken houses serve as a reminder of not only the fact that He set me free from the prison of witchcraft but also that He has used the very thing that looks like a prison from the outside to grow and advance His kingdom through our ministry.

My hope and prayer for you is that you would take a personal inventory of your life. Here are some questions to guide you in this process:

1. What areas of discontentment currently exist in your life? These can be past situations that still fuel discontentment or current ones.

2. Have any of these situations led to positive outcomes? If so, in what ways?

3. What good things has God placed in your life for which you should be thankful?

4. How might you use the circumstances, life events, and material in this book to further realize your purpose in the Lord?

I hope and pray that you will spend intentional time considering and praying through these questions. When we realize our purpose in the Lord and live accordingly, He blesses not only the people to whom we minister, but He blesses us as well. When I realized my purpose to minister to the Muslim community, God revealed things to me I had not previously known. There was a Muslim couple who came to me relatively early in my ministry seeking counsel for their relationship. During this time of counseling, the Holy Spirit revealed to me that they had each been having affairs in their dreams during the previous couple weeks. I told them that I knew what had happened, and this took them by great surprise. They asked me how I knew, and I told them that the Holy Spirit revealed it to me and that Jesus Christ was alive and loved them. I prayed for them, commanded the demons to leave that were causing the problems, and led them to Christ. When we realize our purpose in Christ and live accordingly, He will do amazing things in and through us.

Better realizing our purpose in the Lord is a worthwhile endeavor. On a personal level, it leads to a more trustworthy, fulfilling, and exciting relationship with the Lord. The more we realize our purpose, the more we see God place us in situations where He works in tangible and powerful ways for the glory of His Kingdom. When this happens, it benefits not only us but also those with whom we come in contact. Salvation occurs, lives are changed, and God receives His due praise and glory. I encourage you to pursue your God-given purpose and live fully in the favor that comes with being a child of the Most High King, Jesus Christ.

In Christ,
Muwanga

scripture reference list

NKJV

Foreword

1. Ephesians 6:12

> For we do not wrestle against flesh and blood, but against principalities, against powers, against the rulers of the darkness of this age, against spiritual hosts of wickedness in the heavenly places.

Chapter 4

2. Isaiah 45:1–2

> "Thus says the LORD to His anointed,
> To Cyrus, whose right hand I have held—
> To subdue nations before him
> And loose the armor of kings,
> To open before him the double doors,
> So that the gates will not be shut:
> 'I will go before you
> And make the crooked places straight;
> I will break in pieces the gates of bronze
> And cut the bars of iron.

3. Jeremiah 51:20–24

"You are My battle-ax and weapons of war:
For with you I will break the nation in pieces;
With you I will destroy kingdoms;
With you I will break in pieces the horse and its rider;
With you I will break in pieces the chariot and its rider;
With you also I will break in pieces man and woman;
With you I will break in pieces old and young;
With you I will break in pieces the young man and the maiden;
With you also I will break in pieces the shepherd and his flock;
With you I will break in pieces the farmer and his yoke of oxen;
And with you I will break in pieces governors and rulers.

"And I will repay Babylon
And all the inhabitants of Chaldea
For all the evil they have done
In Zion in your sight," says the LORD.

Chapter 6

4. Isaiah 54:17

"No weapon formed against you shall prosper,
And every tongue which rises against you in judgment
You shall condemn.
This is the heritage of the servants of the LORD,
And their righteousness is from Me,"
Says the LORD.

5. Matthew 5:11–12

"Blessed are you when they revile and persecute you, and say all kinds of evil against you falsely for My sake. Rejoice and be exceedingly glad, for great is your reward in heaven, for so they persecuted the prophets who were before you.

6. Mark 10:29–30

> So Jesus answered and said, "Assuredly, I say to you, there is no one who has left house or brothers or sisters or father or mother or wife or children or lands, for My sake and the gospel's, who shall not receive a hundredfold now in this time—houses and brothers and sisters and mothers and children and lands, with persecutions—and in the age to come, eternal life.

Chapter 7

7. Genesis 3:1–7

> Now the serpent was more cunning than any beast of the field which the LORD God had made. And he said to the woman, "Has God indeed said, 'You shall not eat of every tree of the garden'?"
>
> And the woman said to the serpent, "We may eat the fruit of the trees of the garden; but of the fruit of the tree which is in the midst of the garden, God has said, 'You shall not eat it, nor shall you touch it, lest you die.'"
>
> Then the serpent said to the woman, "You will not surely die. For God knows that in the day you eat of it your eyes will be opened, and you will be like God, knowing good and evil."
>
> So when the woman saw that the tree was good for food, that it was pleasant to the eyes, and a tree desirable to make one wise, she took of its fruit and ate. She also gave to her husband with her, and he ate. Then the eyes of both of them were opened, and they knew that they were naked; and they sewed fig leaves together and made themselves coverings.

8. 2 Timothy 1:7

> For God has not given us a spirit of fear, but of power and of love and of a sound mind.

9. Mark 14:66–72

    Now as Peter was below in the courtyard, one of the servant girls of the high priest came. And when she saw Peter warming himself, she looked at him and said, "You also were with Jesus of Nazareth."

    But he denied it, saying, "I neither know nor understand what you are saying." And he went out on the porch, and a rooster crowed.

    And the servant girl saw him again, and began to say to those who stood by, "This is one of them." But he denied it again.

    And a little later those who stood by said to Peter again, "Surely you are one of them; for you are a Galilean, and your speech shows it."

    Then he began to curse and swear, "I do not know this Man of whom you speak!"

    A second time the rooster crowed. Then Peter called to mind the word that Jesus had said to him, "Before the rooster crows twice, you will deny Me three times." And when he thought about it, he wept.

10. John 1:42

    And he brought him to Jesus.

    Now when Jesus looked at him, He said, "You are Simon the son of Jonah. You shall be called Cephas" (which is translated, A Stone).

*Other translations directly indicate the name change to "Peter":

- He brought him to Jesus. Jesus looked at him and said, "You are Simon the son of John. You shall be called Cephas" (which means Peter). (ESV)
- He brought him to Jesus. Jesus looked at him and said, "You are Simon the son of John; you shall be called Cephas" (which is translated Peter). (NASB)
- And he brought him to Jesus.
  Jesus looked at him and said, "You are Simon son of John. You will be called Cephas" (which, when translated, is Peter). (NIV)

11. Mark 14:31

> But he spoke more vehemently, "If I have to die with You, I will not deny You!"

> And they all said likewise.

12. Mark 10:28–30

> Then Peter began to say to Him, "See, we have left all and followed You."

> So Jesus answered and said, "Assuredly, I say to you, there is no one who has left house or brothers or sisters or father or mother or wife or children or lands, for My sake and the gospel's, who shall not receive a hundredfold now in this time—houses and brothers and sisters and mothers and children and lands, with persecutions—and in the age to come, eternal life.

13. Matthew 5:12

> Rejoice and be exceedingly glad, for great is your reward in heaven, for so they persecuted the prophets who were before you.

14. Matthew 28:19–20

> Go therefore and make disciples of all the nations, baptizing them in the name of the Father and of the Son and of the Holy Spirit, teaching them to observe all things that I have commanded you; and lo, I am with you always, even to the end of the age." men.

Chapter 11

15. Genesis 15:1–21

> After these things the word of the LORD came to Abram in a vision, saying, "Do not be afraid, Abram. I am your shield, your exceedingly great reward."

> But Abram said, "Lord GOD, what will You give me, seeing I go child-

less, and the heir of my house is Eliezer of Damascus?" Then Abram said, "Look, You have given me no offspring; indeed one born in my house is my heir!"

And behold, the word of the LORD came to him, saying, "This one shall not be your heir, but one who will come from your own body shall be your heir." Then He brought him outside and said, "Look now toward heaven, and count the stars if you are able to number them." And He said to him, "So shall your descendants be."

And he believed in the LORD, and He accounted it to him for righteousness.

Then He said to him, "I am the LORD, who brought you out of Ur of the Chaldeans, to give you this land to inherit it."

And he said, "Lord GOD, how shall I know that I will inherit it?"

So He said to him, "Bring Me a three-year-old heifer, a three-year-old female goat, a three-year-old ram, a turtledove, and a young pigeon." Then he brought all these to Him and cut them in two, down the middle, and placed each piece opposite the other; but he did not cut the birds in two. And when the vultures came down on the carcasses, Abram drove them away.

Now when the sun was going down, a deep sleep fell upon Abram; and behold, horror and great darkness fell upon him. Then He said to Abram: "Know certainly that your descendants will be strangers in a land that is not theirs, and will serve them, and they will afflict them four hundred years. And also the nation whom they serve I will judge; afterward they shall come out with great possessions. Now as for you, you shall go to your fathers in peace; you shall be buried at a good old age. But in the fourth generation they shall return here, for the iniquity of the Amorites is not yet complete."

And it came to pass, when the sun went down and it was dark, that behold, there appeared a smoking oven and a burning torch that passed between those pieces. On the same day the LORD made a covenant with Abram, saying:

"To your descendants I have given this land, from the river of Egypt to the great river, the River Euphrates—the Kenites, the Kenezzites, the Kadmonites, the Hittites, the Perizzites, the Rephaim, the Amorites, the Canaanites, the Girgashites, and the Jebusites."

16. Genesis 17:1–5

When Abram was ninety-nine years old, the LORD appeared to Abram and said to him, "I am Almighty God; walk before Me and be blameless. And I will make My covenant between Me and you, and will multiply you exceedingly." Then Abram fell on his face, and God talked with him, saying: "As for Me, behold, My covenant is with you, and you shall be a father of many nations. No longer shall your name be called Abram, but your name shall be Abraham; for I have made you a father of many nations.

17. Genesis 16:1–16

Now Sarai, Abram's wife, had borne him no children. And she had an Egyptian maidservant whose name was Hagar. So Sarai said to Abram, "See now, the LORD has restrained me from bearing children. Please, go in to my maid; perhaps I shall obtain children by her." And Abram heeded the voice of Sarai. Then Sarai, Abram's wife, took Hagar her maid, the Egyptian, and gave her to her husband Abram to be his wife, after Abram had dwelt ten years in the land of Canaan. So he went in to Hagar, and she conceived. And when she saw that she had conceived, her mistress became despised in her eyes.

Then Sarai said to Abram, "My wrong be upon you! I gave my maid into your embrace; and when she saw that she had conceived, I became despised in her eyes. The LORD judge between you and me."

So Abram said to Sarai, "Indeed your maid is in your hand; do to her as you please." And when Sarai dealt harshly with her, she fled from her presence.

Now the Angel of the LORD found her by a spring of water in the wilderness, by the spring on the way to Shur. And He said, "Hagar, Sarai's maid, where have you come from, and where are you going?"

She said, "I am fleeing from the presence of my mistress Sarai."

The Angel of the LORD said to her, "Return to your mistress, and submit yourself under her hand." Then the Angel of the LORD said to her, "I will multiply your descendants exceedingly, so that they shall not be counted for multitude." And the Angel of the LORD said to her:

"Behold, you are with child,
And you shall bear a son.
You shall call his name Ishmael,
Because the LORD has heard your affliction.
He shall be a wild man;
His hand shall be against every man,
And every man's hand against him.
And he shall dwell in the presence of all his brethren."

Then she called the name of the LORD who spoke to her, You-Are-the-God-Who-Sees; for she said, "Have I also here seen Him who sees me?" Therefore the well was called Beer Lahai Roi; observe, it is between Kadesh and Bered.

So Hagar bore Abram a son; and Abram named his son, whom Hagar bore, Ishmael. Abram was eighty-six years old when Hagar bore Ishmael to Abram.

18. 1 John 4:1

Beloved, do not believe every spirit, but test the spirits, whether they are of God; because many false prophets have gone out into the world.

19. Luke 6:32

But if you love those who love you, what credit is that to you? For even sinners love those who love them.

Chapter 12

20. Genesis 1:1

In the beginning God created the heavens and the earth.

21. Genesis 1:28

Then God blessed them, and God said to them, "Be fruitful and multiply; fill the earth and subdue it; have dominion over the fish of the sea, over the birds of the air, and over every living thing that moves on the earth."

22. Genesis 2:18

And the LORD God said, "It is not good that man should be alone; I will make him a helper comparable to him."

23. Genesis 2:22

Then the rib which the LORD God had taken from man He made into a woman, and He brought her to the man.

24. Genesis 1:1

In the beginning God created the heavens and the earth.

25. John 3:16

For God so loved the world that He gave His only begotten Son, that whoever believes in Him should not perish but have everlasting life.

26. Romans 8:11

But if the Spirit of Him who raised Jesus from the dead dwells in you, He who raised Christ from the dead will also give life to your mortal bodies through His Spirit who dwells in you.

27. John 16:7–11

Nevertheless I tell you the truth. It is to your advantage that I go away; for if I do not go away, the Helper will not come to you; but if I depart, I will send Him to you. And when He has come, He will convict the world of sin, and of righteousness, and of judgment: of sin, because they do not believe in Me; of righteousness, because I go to My Father and you see Me no more; of judgment, because the ruler of this world is judged.

28. Romans 15:16

that I might be a minister of Jesus Christ to the Gentiles, ministering the gospel of God, that the offering of the Gentiles might be acceptable, sanctified by the Holy Spirit.

29. Galatians 5:16–24

I say then: Walk in the Spirit, and you shall not fulfill the lust of the flesh. For the flesh lusts against the Spirit, and the Spirit against the flesh; and these are contrary to one another, so that you do not do the things that you wish. But if you are led by the Spirit, you are not under the law.

Now the works of the flesh are evident, which are: adultery, fornication, uncleanness, lewdness, idolatry, sorcery, hatred, contentions, jealousies, outbursts of wrath, selfish ambitions, dissensions, heresies, envy, murders, drunkenness, revelries, and the like; of which I tell you beforehand, just as I also told you in time past, that those who practice such things will not inherit the kingdom of God.

But the fruit of the Spirit is love, joy, peace, longsuffering, kindness, goodness, faithfulness, gentleness, self-control. Against such there is no law. And those who are Christ's have crucified the flesh with its passions and desires.

30. Romans 8:26

Likewise the Spirit also helps in our weaknesses. For we do not know what we should pray for as we ought, but the Spirit Himself makes intercession for us with groanings which cannot be uttered.

31. Isaiah 14:13

For you have said in your heart:
'I will ascend into heaven,
I will exalt my throne above the stars of God;
I will also sit on the mount of the congregation
On the farthest sides of the north;

32. Isaiah 14:14

I will ascend above the heights of the clouds,
I will be like the Most High.'

33. Genesis 2:16–17

And the LORD God commanded the man, saying, "Of every tree of the garden you may freely eat; but of the tree of the knowledge of good and evil you shall not eat, for in the day that you eat of it you shall surely die."

34. Genesis 3:1–5

Now the serpent was more cunning than any beast of the field which the

LORD God had made. And he said to the woman, "Has God indeed said, 'You shall not eat of every tree of the garden'?"

And the woman said to the serpent, "We may eat the fruit of the trees of the garden; but of the fruit of the tree which is in the midst of the garden, God has said, 'You shall not eat it, nor shall you touch it, lest you die.'"

Then the serpent said to the woman, "You will not surely die. For God knows that in the day you eat of it your eyes will be opened, and you will be like God, knowing good and evil."

35. Genesis 3:6

So when the woman saw that the tree was good for food, that it was pleasant to the eyes, and a tree desirable to make one wise, she took of its fruit and ate. She also gave to her husband with her, and he ate.

36. Romans 6:23

For the wages of sin is death, but the gift of God is eternal life in Christ Jesus our Lord.

37. Luke 7:41–43

"A certain moneylender had two debtors. One owed five hundred denarii, and the other fifty. When they could not pay, he cancelled the debt of both. Now which of them will love him more?" Simon answered, "The one, I suppose, for whom he cancelled the larger debt." And he said to him, "You have judged rightly."

38. 1 Corinthians 15:20–22

But now Christ is risen from the dead, and has become the firstfruits of those who have fallen asleep. For since by man came death, by Man also came the resurrection of the dead. For as in Adam all die, even so in Christ all shall be made alive.

39. Colossians 1:20

and by Him to reconcile all things to Himself, by Him, whether things on earth or things in heaven, having made peace through the blood of His cross.

40. John 14:6

   Jesus said to him, "I am the way, the truth, and the life. No one comes to the Father except through Me."

41. Romans 5:10–11

   For if when we were enemies we were reconciled to God through the death of His Son, much more, having been reconciled, we shall be saved by His life. And not only that, but we also rejoice in God through our Lord Jesus Christ, through whom we have now received the reconciliation.

42. John 6:44

   No one can come to Me unless the Father who sent Me draws him; and I will raise him up at the last day.

43. Romans 5:10–11

   For if when we were enemies we were reconciled to God through the death of His Son, much more, having been reconciled, we shall be saved by His life. And not only that, but we also rejoice in God through our Lord Jesus Christ, through whom we have now received the reconciliation.

44. 1 Peter 3:18

   For Christ also suffered once for sins, the just for the unjust, that He might bring us to God, being put to death in the flesh but made alive by the Spirit,

45. 2 Corinthians 1:21–22

   Now He who establishes us with you in Christ and has anointed us is God, who also has sealed us and given us the Spirit in our hearts as a guarantee.

46. Revelation 21:1–4

   Now I saw a new heaven and a new earth, for the first heaven and the first earth had passed away. Also there was no more sea. Then I, John, saw the holy city, New Jerusalem, coming down out of heaven from God, prepared as a bride adorned for her husband. And I heard a loud voice from heaven saying, "Behold, the tabernacle of God is with men, and He will dwell with them, and they shall be His people. God

Himself will be with them and be their God. And God will wipe away every tear from their eyes; there shall be no more death, nor sorrow, nor crying. There shall be no more pain, for the former things have passed away."

47. Revelation 21:5

Then He who sat on the throne said, "Behold, I make all things new." And He said to me, "Write, for these words are true and faithful."

Chapter 13

48. 1 Peter 5:8

Be sober, be vigilant; because your adversary the devil walks about like a roaring lion, seeking whom he may devour.

49. Proverbs 23:29–35

Who has woe?
Who has sorrow?
Who has contentions?
Who has complaints?
Who has wounds without cause?
Who has redness of eyes?
Those who linger long at the wine,
Those who go in search of mixed wine.
Do not look on the wine when it is red,
When it sparkles in the cup,
When it swirls around smoothly;
At the last it bites like a serpent,
And stings like a viper.
Your eyes will see strange things,
And your heart will utter perverse things.
Yes, you will be like one who lies down in the midst of the sea,
Or like one who lies at the top of the mast, saying:
"They have struck me, but I was not hurt;
They have beaten me, but I did not feel it.
When shall I awake, that I may seek another drink?"

Chapter 15

50. Acts 2:2

   And suddenly there came a sound from heaven, as of a rushing mighty wind, and it filled the whole house where they were sitting.

51. Acts 2:4

   And they were all filled with the Holy Spirit and began to speak with other tongues, as the Spirit gave them utterance.

52. Acts 2:12

   So they were all amazed and perplexed, saying to one another, "Whatever could this mean?"

53. Acts 2:42–47

   And they continued steadfastly in the apostles' doctrine and fellowship, in the breaking of bread, and in prayers. Then fear came upon every soul, and many wonders and signs were done through the apostles. Now all who believed were together, and had all things in common, and sold their possessions and goods, and divided them among all, as anyone had need.

   So continuing daily with one accord in the temple, and breaking bread from house to house, they ate their food with gladness and simplicity of heart, praising God and having favor with all the people. And the Lord added to the church daily those who were being saved.

54. 1 Corinthians 12:4–11

   There are diversities of gifts, but the same Spirit. There are differences of ministries, but the same Lord. And there are diversities of activities, but it is the same God who works all in all. But the manifestation of the Spirit is given to each one for the profit of all: for to one is given the word of wisdom through the Spirit, to another the word of knowledge through the same Spirit, to another faith by the same Spirit, to another gifts of healings by the same Spirit, to another the working of miracles, to another prophecy, to another discerning of spirits, to another different kinds of tongues, to another the interpretation of tongues. But one and the same Spirit works all these things, distributing to each one individually as He wills.

55. Romans 8:26

Likewise the Spirit also helps in our weaknesses. For we do not know what we should pray for as we ought, but the Spirit Himself makes intercession for us with groanings which cannot be uttered.

56. Acts 4:12

Nor is there salvation in any other, for there is no other name under heaven given among men by which we must be saved."

57. Romans 10:9

that if you confess with your mouth the Lord Jesus and believe in your heart that God has raised Him from the dead, you will be saved.

58. John 14:12

Most assuredly, I say to you, he who believes in Me, the works that I do he will do also; and greater works than these he will do, because I go to My Father.

59. Philippians 2:10

that at the name of Jesus every knee should bow, of those in heaven, and of those on earth, and of those under the earth

60. Mark 11:23–24

For assuredly, I say to you, whoever says to this mountain, 'Be removed and be cast into the sea,' and does not doubt in his heart, but believes that those things he says will be done, he will have whatever he says. Therefore I say to you, whatever things you ask when you pray, believe that you receive them, and you will have them.

61. Hebrews 12:24

to Jesus the Mediator of the new covenant, and to the blood of sprinkling that speaks better things than that of Abel.

62. Hebrews 4:12

For the word of God is living and powerful, and sharper than any two-edged sword, piercing even to the division of soul and spirit, and of joints and marrow, and is a discerner of the thoughts and intents of the heart.

63. John 1:1

In the beginning was the Word, and the Word was with God, and the Word was God.

64. John 8:31

Then Jesus said to those Jews who believed Him, "If you abide in My word, you are My disciples indeed.

65. John 10:28–29

And I give them eternal life, and they shall never perish; neither shall anyone snatch them out of My hand. My Father, who has given them to Me, is greater than all; and no one is able to snatch them out of My Father's hand.

66. John 15:4–5

Abide in Me, and I in you. As the branch cannot bear fruit of itself, unless it abides in the vine, neither can you, unless you abide in Me.

"I am the vine, you are the branches. He who abides in Me, and I in him, bears much fruit; for without Me you can do nothing.

67. John 15:10

If you keep My commandments, you will abide in My love, just as I have kept My Father's commandments and abide in His love.

68. 1 John 3:6

Whoever abides in Him does not sin. Whoever sins has neither seen Him nor known Him.

69. 1 John 3:24

Now he who keeps His commandments abides in Him, and He in him. And by this we know that He abides in us, by the Spirit whom He has given us.

70. 1 John 4:13

By this we know that we abide in Him, and He in us, because He has given us of His Spirit.

71. Genesis 3:1–5

Now the serpent was more cunning than any beast of the field which the

LORD God had made. And he said to the woman, "Has God indeed said, 'You shall not eat of every tree of the garden'?"

And the woman said to the serpent, "We may eat the fruit of the trees of the garden; but of the fruit of the tree which is in the midst of the garden, God has said, 'You shall not eat it, nor shall you touch it, lest you die.'"

Then the serpent said to the woman, "You will not surely die. For God knows that in the day you eat of it your eyes will be opened, and you will be like God, knowing good and evil."

72. Genesis 3:6

So when the woman saw that the tree was good for food, that it was pleasant to the eyes, and a tree desirable to make one wise, she took of its fruit and ate. She also gave to her husband with her, and he ate.

73. Matthew 4:1–11

Then Jesus was led up by the Spirit into the wilderness to be tempted by the devil. And when He had fasted forty days and forty nights, afterward He was hungry. Now when the tempter came to Him, he said, "If You are the Son of God, command that these stones become bread."

But He answered and said, "It is written, 'Man shall not live by bread alone, but by every word that proceeds from the mouth of God.'"

Then the devil took Him up into the holy city, set Him on the pinnacle of the temple, and said to Him, "If You are the Son of God, throw Yourself down. For it is written:

'He shall give His angels charge over you,'
and,
'In their hands they shall bear you up,
Lest you dash your foot against a stone.'"

Jesus said to him, "It is written again, 'You shall not tempt the LORD your God.'"

Again, the devil took Him up on an exceedingly high mountain, and showed Him all the kingdoms of the world and their glory. And he said to Him, "All these things I will give You if You will fall down and worship me."

Then Jesus said to him, "Away with you, Satan! For it is written, 'You shall worship the LORD your God, and Him only you shall serve.'"

Then the devil left Him, and behold, angels came and ministered to Him.

74. Hebrews 4:12

For the word of God is living and powerful, and sharper than any two-edged sword, piercing even to the division of soul and spirit, and of joints and marrow, and is a discerner of the thoughts and intents of the heart.

75. Matthew 28:19–20

Go therefore and make disciples of all the nations, baptizing them in the name of the Father and of the Son and of the Holy Spirit, teaching them to observe all things that I have commanded you; and lo, I am with you always, even to the end of the age." Amen.

Chapter 16

76. Philippians 2:8

And being found in appearance as a man, He humbled Himself and became obedient to the point of death, even the death of the cross.

77. Matthew 7:11

If you then, being evil, know how to give good gifts to your children, how much more will your Father who is in heaven give good things to those who ask Him!

78. James 1:17

Every good gift and every perfect gift is from above, and comes down from the Father of lights, with whom there is no variation or shadow of turning.

79. Matthew 6:9–13:

In this manner, therefore, pray:
Our Father in heaven,

Hallowed be Your name.
Your kingdom come.
Your will be done
On earth as it is in heaven.
Give us this day our daily bread.
And forgive us our debts,
As we forgive our debtors.
And do not lead us into temptation,
But deliver us from the evil one.
For Yours is the kingdom and the power and the glory forever. Amen.

80. 2 Chronicles 7:14

if My people who are called by My name will humble themselves, and pray and seek My face, and turn from their wicked ways, then I will hear from heaven, and will forgive their sin and heal their land.

81. Psalm 34:17

The righteous cry out, and the LORD hears,
And delivers them out of all their troubles.

82. Mark 1:35

Now in the morning, having risen a long while before daylight, He went out and departed to a solitary place; and there He prayed.

83. Luke 11:9

So I say to you, ask, and it will be given to you; seek, and you will find; knock, and it will be opened to you.

84. John 16:23–24

And in that day you will ask Me nothing. Most assuredly, I say to you, whatever you ask the Father in My name He will give you. Until now you have asked nothing in My name. Ask, and you will receive, that your joy may be full.

85. Ephesians 6:18

praying always with all prayer and supplication in the Spirit, being watchful to this end with all perseverance and supplication for all the saints

86. James 5:16

Confess your trespasses to one another, and pray for one another, that you may be healed. The effective, fervent prayer of a righteous man avails much.

87. Mark 1:35–38

Now in the morning, having risen a long while before daylight, He went out and departed to a solitary place; and there He prayed. And Simon and those who were with Him searched for Him. When they found Him, they said to Him, "Everyone is looking for You."

But He said to them, "Let us go into the next towns, that I may preach there also, because for this purpose I have come forth."

88. Luke 1:37

For with God nothing will be impossible.

89. Ephesians 6:18

praying always with all prayer and supplication in the Spirit, being watchful to this end with all perseverance and supplication for all the saints—

90. James 5:16

Confess your trespasses to one another, and pray for one another, that you may be healed. The effective, fervent prayer of a righteous man avails much.

91. 2 Corinthians 10:5

casting down arguments and every high thing that exalts itself against the knowledge of God, bringing every thought into captivity to the obedience of Christ,

92. Romans 8:26–27

Likewise the Spirit also helps in our weaknesses. For we do not know what we should pray for as we ought, but the Spirit Himself makes intercession for us with groanings which cannot be uttered. Now He who searches the hearts knows what the mind of the Spirit is, because He makes intercession for the saints according to the will of God.

93. Romans 8:28

And we know that all things work together for good to those who love God, to those who are the called according to His purpose.

94. Romans 8:37

Yet in all these things we are more than conquerors through Him who loved us.

95. 1 Peter 2:24

who Himself bore our sins in His own body on the tree, that we, having died to sins, might live for righteousness—by whose stripes you were healed

96. 1 Corinthians 6:19

Or do you not know that your body is the temple of the Holy Spirit who is in you, whom you have from God, and you are not your own?

97. Matthew 7:7–11

"Ask, and it will be given to you; seek, and you will find; knock, and it will be opened to you. For everyone who asks receives, and he who seeks finds, and to him who knocks it will be opened. Or what man is there among you who, if his son asks for bread, will give him a stone? Or if he asks for a fish, will he give him a serpent? If you then, being evil, know how to give good gifts to your children, how much more will your Father who is in heaven give good things to those who ask Him!

Chapter 17

98. Hebrews 4:12

For the word of God is living and powerful, and sharper than any two-edged sword, piercing even to the division of soul and spirit, and of joints and marrow, and is a discerner of the thoughts and intents of the heart.

99. Philippians 3:10

For the word of God is living and powerful, and sharper than any two-edged sword, piercing even to the division of soul and spirit, and of joints and marrow, and is a discerner of the thoughts and intents of the heart.

100. Ephesians 2:8–10

For by grace you have been saved through faith, and that not of your-selves; it is the gift of God, not of works, lest anyone should boast. For we are His workmanship, created in Christ Jesus for good works, which God prepared beforehand that we should walk in them.

101. James 1:14–15 (NKJV)

But each one is tempted when he is drawn away by his own desires and enticed. Then, when desire has conceived, it gives birth to sin; and sin, when it is full-grown, brings forth death.

102. Matthew 6:16–18

Moreover, when you fast, do not be like the hypocrites, with a sad countenance. For they disfigure their faces that they may appear to men to be fasting. Assuredly, I say to you, they have their reward. But you, when you fast, anoint your head and wash your face, so that you do not appear to men to be fasting, but to your Father who is in the secret place; and your Father who sees in secret will reward you openly.

103. 1 Corinthians 9:27

But I discipline my body and bring it into subjection, lest, when I have preached to others, I myself should become disqualified.

104. Matthew 4:1–2

Then Jesus was led up by the Spirit into the wilderness to be tempted by the devil. And when He had fasted forty days and forty nights, after-ward He was hungry.

105. Luke 4:1–2

Then Jesus, being filled with the Holy Spirit, returned from the Jordan and was led by the Spirit into the wilderness, being tempted for forty days by the devil. And in those days He ate nothing, and afterward, when they had ended, He was hungry.

citations

1. Salvation definition: https://en.oxforddictionaries.com/defini-
   tion/salvation

2. World Religion Map: http://d3tt741pwxqwm0.cloudfront.net/
   WGBH/sj14/sj14-int-religmap/index.html

3. Qureshi, Nabeel. Seeking Allah, Finding Jesus: A Devout Muslim
   Encounters Christianity. Grand Rapids, MI: Zondervan, 2018.

4. *Quran,* trans. Talal Itani. God Edition, found at https://www.
   clearquran.com.

5. *Sahih Bukhari*, trans. M. Muhsin Khan, found at www.sacred-
   texts.com/isl/bukhari/bh4/index.htm.

Printed in the USA
CPSIA information can be obtained
at www.ICGtesting.com
LVHW021548131023
760943LV00049B/1199